On Your Mark . . .
Get Set
Go!
Destination Uganda

Ivy Otto

Copyright @2018 Ivy Otto

All rights reserved.

ISBN-13: 978-1725832473

ISBN-10: 172583247X

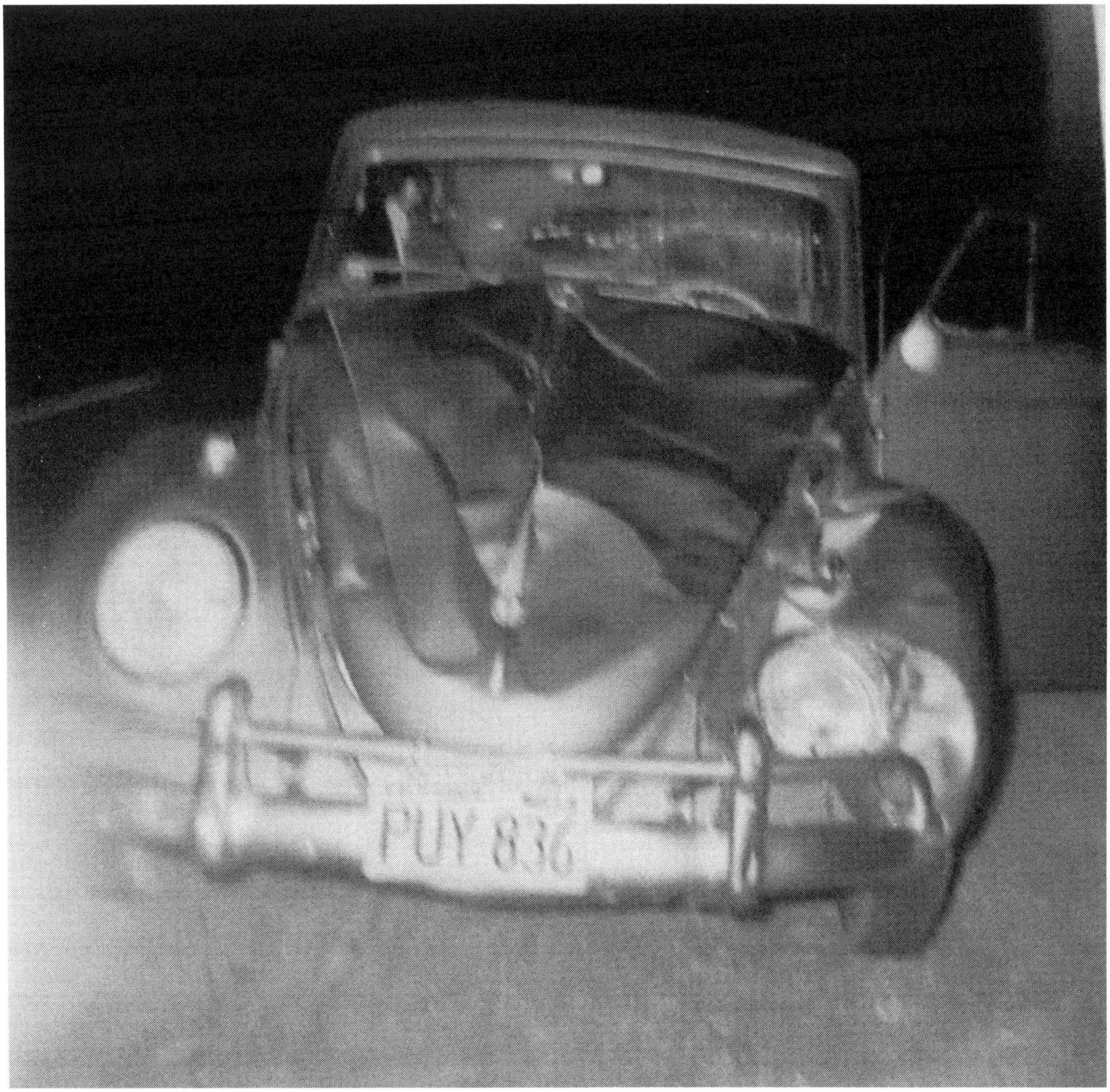
PUY 836

DEDICATION

To my husband and best friend and my three wonderful kids!

PREFACE

I find autobiographies engrossing. Oh, not all life-stories are by any means equally interesting. And certainly, not even those written by Christians are spiritually edifying. But this account of a woman's faith-journey is both engrossing and edifying. Ivy's detailed self-narrative deserves a prominent place in the literature of missionary ministry. And the lessons she learned in the crucible of both humdrum and heroic service are lessons every believer needs to learn. Here is material enough for a half-dozen novels—except that Ivy's story is not fiction. It is instead in the highest sense a redemptive romance. It tells how God's love for a 20th century Colorado girl inspired her and the husband she loves to share the love of Bethlehem and Calvary with people far from Colorado for whom in love Jesus died.

-Dr. Vernon Grounds

TABLE OF CONTENTS

FORWARD
ACKNOWLEDGEMENTS
INTRODUCTION

PART I – ON YOUR MARK . . .
    CHAPTER 1 – WHAT CAN PARENTS DO? - 7
    CHAPTER 2 – GOD CONFRONTS ME - 15
    CHAPTER 3 – POINT OF NO RETURN - 17
    CHAPTER 4 – GOD'S UNDERSHEPHERDS - 22
    CHAPTER 5 – WHAT HAS GOD GIVEN? - 28
    CHAPTER 6 – CAN SCHOOL HELP? - 32
    CHAPTER 7 – HAWAII – A STEPPING STONE - 39

PART II – GET SET
    CHAPTER 8 – WEAKNESS TO BECOME STRONG - 46
    CHAPTER 9 – MORE TESTS - 54
    CHAPTER 10 – GOD SOLVES MY BIGGEST PROBLEM - 60
    CHAPTER 11 – SURVIVING SEMINARY - 75

PART III – GO!
    CHAPTER 12 – FINALLY TO UGANDA - 86
    CHAPTER 13 – CHAOS IN UGANDA - 92
    CHAPTER 14 – R & R IN AMERICA - 105
    CHAPTER 15 – WAR IN UGANDA - 120
    CHAPTER 16 – REAPPOINTMENT TO AFRICA - 136
    CHAPTER 17 – GOD AT WORK IN UGANDA - 143
    CHAPTER 18 – NEAR DEATH IN COLORADO - 160
    CHAPTER 19 – LOSSES IN UGANDA - 168
    CHAPTER 20 – HOME ASSIGNMENT - 182
    CHAPTER 21 – GOD'S REWARDS - 192
    CHAPTER 22 – PRAISE - 197

    EPILOGUE - 203

FOREWARD

*"You did not choose me, but I chose
you to go and bear fruit — fruit that
will last." John15:16.*

Have you ever felt your life was so full you'd pop? So blessed by God that the tears of joy could not be restrained? And as you look back, do you realize what often seemed bad at the time has turned into the biggest and best blessing you could ever imagine? Don't you wish you'd anticipated a little of the joy that lay ahead so the present would have been more tolerable?

Hey! That's what Christianity is all about! Faith! We must believe God is making us like Christ. Oh, that our faith would be big enough for us to know confidently that this is what God is doing — filling our lives with *real* joy and inexpressible satisfaction. That walking with God is not only *the* way but the *happiest* way!

Getting ready must begin with the precious truth that *God* has chosen us for the race. With choosing us, He brings experiences and circumstances into our lives to guide us in the way He wants us to go.

When I was a senior in high school my English teacher asked the class to write an autobiography. The last chapter was entitled, "What I Expect to Accomplish by the Time I'm Fifty." Of course, that manuscript expressed the dreams most youth have. My dream was to be happily married to a preacher, have a famous quartet comprised of our four sons, and yes, you guessed it — to have three girls, again all singers. This magnanimous family lived in the Colorado Rockies, pastoring a small church there. The boys were athletes and the girls, cheerleaders, exactly as I had dreamed, but better!

What I have learned is although I had my dreams, my life was to be "What *God* Expected to Accomplish by the Time I was Fifty." I have looked back over my life and realized that He has given me bigger and better things than my dream could ever have been. He chose me and chose the path for my life. "DESTINATION UGANDA" is the story of my life and how God has accomplished His purpose in it and blessed me beyond words. He knew what would put me on the mark; what training I needed to get set; and finally what needed to happen so I could go . . . to Uganda.

ACKNOWLEDGEMENTS

God planted the idea for this book in my mind, but I must thank all the people that had a part in helping me complete that idea. Mainly, I need to thank all the people that had a part in my life. Special thanks goes to Uncle Paul Eiselstein for the things he taught me. Without the encouragement of my husband, I know I would not have finished this assignment. My son, Tim, bought me books to help me and urged me to push on. Of course, there were the prayers and encouragement of Nancy and Julie, my daughters.

I also extend thanks to Dr. Grounds for the preface, to Ed Stewart and his kind counsel. Without the wise counsel of Dr. Ralph Covell, the book would have had little focus and not revealed the message I wanted to share. And finally, I give my heartfelt thanks to Rosemary Savone, my editor. Without her, this work would never have been accomplished and would contain mistakes enough to discourage everyone from reading it!

Thanks to *Psalms Now* by Leslie Brandt, copyright 1973 by Concordia Publishing House. Reproduced with permission under license number 99:11-100.

INTRODUCTION

It was a beautiful day in Hawaii. The sun was shining, the air balmy and warm. But I was hot, unaware of the outward world. I wandered through a strange maze of memory. I recalled the snowy slopes of Camp Id-Ra-Ha-Je. I saw my sister, Laura, crash into a tree, fall from the toboggan, and lie there as if dead. Why was I remembering this? I hadn't even been with my sister when she had that accident. I'd only been told what had happened. I felt the bit of cold on my throat and covered my mouth to warm the icy air. I jerked my hand away. I was not cold but very hot!

Slowly the present came back. There was no snow. I was hot because I was running a very high temperature. Was that my friend, Shirley, I could hear? Why, yes, she was asking me what she could do to help me. I opened my eyes to the bare room I called home during my three months stay in Maui, Hawaii.

But when I closed my eyes, another vision from my past appeared. I saw a small nine-year-old girl standing, singing, at the front of Camp Id-Ra-Ha-Je Chapel while I played the piano. "The devil is a rustle (***, rustle?), and .. .. ."

"No, no!" I cried.. "He can't have me!"

Snap. Again I gained consciousness and realized I was sick in bed in Hawaii. My mind was calling up small, unrelated glimpses of the past. Nothing made sense.

"Ivy, Ivy! What's wrong?" It was Shirley again.

"I don't know, Shirley. When am I? Oh, forgive me, I do know. But what's wrong with me? My mind keeps taking me back to my childhood and I'm . . . "

I had no strength to talk. My eyes closed, and there was that nine-year-old girl again. "And when the round-up's over, and payday rolls around."

"Lord, is my round-up over?" I asked.

Vaguely I heard Shirley leave the room and scream, "Please, come quick. Ivy's dying!"

My heart was at peace. I had no fear. I knew that in a minute or two I'd be in Jesus' arms. I wasn't anxious to go, but I was ready.

PART I

"ON YOUR MARK . . ."

CHAPTER 1 – WHAT CAN PARENTS DO?

"You did not choose me, but I chose you . . . "
John 15:16

Why God chose me is a mystery I shall never understand but be eternally grateful for! God planted the desire to know Him in my heart at a very young age.

When God chooses you, He begins to slowly move you to a place where He can let you know He loves you and *has chosen* you. He uses circumstances, people, and places to work His plan. In my case, God used non-Christian parents to move me to Him. October 14, 1938 the doctor came to our house. The house was on 1812 Ford Street in Golden, Colorado. Just behind the houses across the street stood Castle Rock – beautiful to see and unique in shape.

Dad was at work but Mom was in labor. That morning Iva Jean Owens entered the world. For 2 weeks, as was the practice in those days, Grandma Petersen cared for Mom as she healed. I will tell you more about that patient mother but for now, let me introduce you to my Dad.

DAD – BILL

Dad was a mean man. I idolized him. He could sing, play the piano by ear, and was hot on the trumpet. In fact, he had his own jazz band that met at our home each week for practice. He was jovial and always joked around. The people of the community loved Bill. He was teased about being Billy Goat who married Nanny Goat (my mom's name was Nan) and had three kids. Dad was special to me because I was his girl! My younger sister, Laura—chubby, redheaded, and happy—was Mom's girl, and my youngest sister, Martha, was "baby."

Having a dad that enjoyed music, I began my love for music. Mom also played the piano a little and encouraged me to learn. I tried piano lessons at age six, but Mom soon found out I wasn't reading the music. I would have the teacher play the song, and then I played it by ear. Mom refused to pay money for something I already knew how to do. So she jerked me out of the lessons, and I continued on my own. Dad also had an interest in helping people. He met some of the poorest and most uneducated of peoples. Many of those were of criminal mind since he was employed at the boy's state reform school in Golden, Colorado, (actually called the Boy's Industrial School.) This was the school to which juvenile delinquents were sent by the courts.

Although he worked the night shift, he knew many of the boys and tried to teach them a trade so they could change their course of life. He knew that unless the boys had some alternatives to a life of crime, they would go out and soon be returned for another act of disobedience. He shared his skills of building and engineering in the boiler room.

Dad worked hard. He usually had more than two jobs—the state job and then other private enterprises. He was the town wallpaper man. He used old-fashioned half-inch thick yardsticks to help spread the paper on the wall. All too often he used one on me if I disobeyed him! I can still remember the gooey taste of wallpaper paste, the sawhorses he hauled around on which he placed the long boards so he could stretch out the paper and put on the glue, and Mom going along to help measure and cut the paper.

Then for a while, Dad had a Raleigh's products route. I think the vanilla flavoring they made was especially good. They also made a salve that healed everything! But my dad enjoyed talking to people much more than selling the product.

Dad had a great influence on me. He taught me how to be interested in other people more than in myself. He had the great social skill of making people feel cared for. I observed these methods of communication and soon learned how to be sociable and made people the center of the conversation. My dad had little trouble making friends, and his happy attitudes were very attractive to me.

Dad's negative attributes also had their effect on me. His quick temper became a part of me, and I experienced many times when my temper ended up being ugly and destructive. I longed to be free of it. In later years I learned that a controlling temper is an attitude that a loving God can forgive and change. I often wish my dad had known that.

I would like to defend my dad. But to help you understand the struggles I have had as a Christian and to let you see the great miracles God has accomplished in my life, I must tell you some of the hard things Dad brought into my life. Because he had such a hot temper, which was usually out of control, he was destructive to both people and things. If a person angered him, he would begin a fight. Many times he beat me until I had to hide the bruises I carried. Today I would be called a physically abused child. I did learn at a very young age to run! By age eight, I could usually outrun Dad and so some of the abuse did stop.

One time when Laura, my sister, was only eight months old, I was watching her in the front yard. We were playing happily together, and I truly loved her. She reached off the blanket and touched a sprinkler from the hose. It was hot from the sun, and she began to cry. I took her in my arms to comfort her. Dad rushed out of the house, grabbed Laura into his arms, and began kicking and beating me! Wasn't I the one that had made her cry? With no questioning he assumed I was the cause of her crying. I was deeply hurt, felt Dad loved Laura more than me, and decided that she was to be hated, not loved. I had to protect myself from future misunderstandings, and I actually became very jealous of Laura.

Most of my friends were also afraid of Dad because they knew, although he could joke and have fun, if he disagreed with you on something, you could receive a fist in the face. If he was trying to repair something and any little thing did not fit or was a bit hard to accomplish, he would break the item by smashing it on the ground or throwing it across the room. Patience was not one of his virtues. Since he handled frustration by breaking things, yelling, and cursing, I learned to handle frustrations the same way. This was my example, and I had no idea of any other way to handle things that seemed beyond me or were contrary to my wishes.

My biggest heartache was to see him use this temper on our soft-spoken Mom. Yes, at times she, in self-defense, would strike out, but Dad was physically stronger than Mom and would hurt her. I saw him beat her; found her lying on the floor with bruises on her face and body. His words were also so strong and hurtful that Mom would run from the verbal abuse that he often gave. I felt suffocated by his anger and was in great fear of him most of my early life.

I never knew how Dad would respond to things I would share with him. Would he be angry about what I shared, would he be pleased, would he ignore me? I never knew, and more often than not he would react completely opposite to what I expected. Once I shared that some town hoodlums with the intent to steal our car had chased five of us from the youth group in a car. We had been able to ditch them but had been very afraid. My dad's reaction was not one of relief that we ended up okay. Instead, he began his abusive verbiage and threw a sharp butcher knife at me. The knife hit my glass of orange juice, shattering the glass and covering me with the juice. But to this day I am thankful the knife did not hit *me!*

Although anger is only one small sin, its results are devastating. Anger creates insecurity, fear, inability to deal with frustrations, and a low self-image. I found it was very hard to please such a person, and usually, I was told how inadequate I was. In turn, I tried to take out my anger, created by false accusations, on someone else. Those smaller than me were usually the recipients. I treated my sisters the way Dad treated me. It is not the right way to build good relationships, and I continually widened the gap of hate, distrust, and anger between my sisters and me.

It became a vicious circle. Dad struck me, I struck my sisters. They then struck out against me, and I would strike back. My low self-image grew because not only did Dad reject me but also my younger sisters rejected me. My insecurity grew because I was sure no one loved me. Mom tried to protect each child, and as she would defend one child, the others would feel rejected. Only a loving forgiving God can correct and change such patterns. I wish our family had known God when we were still at home together.

MOM – NAN

Mom was that quiet, stable, hard-worker that kept our family together. Her creativity was never-ending. The many things she could do amazed me. Born of Danish immigrants in a family of nine, she had to do a lot of work. The family did their own planting, harvesting, grinding, baking, cooking, sewing; working was their way of life. Grandpa died when Mom was sixteen so she and her sister raised the five younger children while Grandma worked outside the home.

The family could afford to send only one child to college. Since Sena was the oldest child, she was given first choice. She decided she wanted to attend college. Mom, the second born, was asked to go to work to contribute to the family income. She was always good in school and wanted desperately to go to college. But she also felt the responsibility of helping the family, so she got a job. However, that didn't stop her from learning. She worked in dress factories and became an outstanding seamstress. There they taught her to work quickly and efficiently. She was a good mathematician, and today her talents in accounting get her many jobs. Although Mom is now eighty, she is the church treasurer, makes clothes—even wedding dresses—for clients, and works in the local women's organization that makes sweaters, quilts, and afghans for orphans and widows.

Because of all this training, her desire to learn, and her initiative, my mom felt anything could be accomplished. "Where there's a will, there's a way," was one of her favorite sayings. Mom made our bread for the week. She canned enough food to last the whole winter season. Because Dad had diabetics, she used saccharine in all the canning. We drove to Grand Junction, 250 miles away, every year to purchase tree-ripe peaches, apricots, and pears which she canned. (Usually about fourteen bushels!) We had popcorn, cucumbers, and other vegetables for the year also. We hardly knew that stores had canned goods. And we certainly didn't know you could go out to eat!

Mom built all the cupboards in our house. In our bedroom she built a special desk, shelves, and drawer set. It was not only very usable but lovely.

Mom made all of the clothes for herself and us three girls. She often made our underwear, our coats, all our dresses—even formal dresses. We actually didn't know you could buy clothes from a store. We learned about that one time when we went on a family fishing trip and forgot our suitcase. We *had* to buy some clothes to wear while we washed the dirty ones!

Mom always felt she could do anything. This value soon became a part of me. When I had a problem and asked her for help, she always said, "You can do it!" As far as I could see, there was nothing Mom couldn't do. I believed her when she said, "People do that; you are a 'people'; you can do it too!" She really believed that and always attempted things on her own and thus her example helped me to have the same attitude.

Mom loved Dad. She loved us. She had come from a family where affection was not openly shown; love was expressed in giving and serving. As a child, I did not recognize her love for me because I desired to be hugged and held. Today I realize how deep Mom's love was, and is, for all of us. It was her faithful love and patience that kept us together as a family and kept her loving an angry man.

God used these parents to build in me values and qualities that He would use in many ways. Although at this time they did not know Him, God was using them. Praise God for every lesson He teaches—for every experience in life. If you are His, you were chosen and He uses all the experiences He allows to come your way for a purpose. God is sovereign!

FAMILY –LAURA – MARTHA

My parents did not attend church, but Dad, raised in the Methodist Church, took me to the Methodist Sunday School. At that particular church the children only played or were kept busy coloring, but somehow I felt it was a good place to be. When I was nine, the family moved four miles from town. I still had the longing to go to Sunday school, but now things were complicated.

Dad said if I wanted to go, I'd have to ride the streetcar and take both younger sisters with me. So with Laura, age five, and Martha, age three, dragging behind, I tried desperately to get them to walk with me the one-half mile to the streetcar. They were so small I had to lift them up into the streetcar and seat them as it rattled along into town. At the other end we had to walk another fourth of a mile up a steep hill to get to the church. What a struggle! Amidst tears, rebellion, and the fatigue of carrying Martha up that hill, I didn't even enjoy Sunday school. By the time we finally got back home, I was dirty, tired, and so angry with the two girls that I decided never to do it again.

But now came the dilemma. I *had* to go to church. When God calls people to Himself, they must answer, and although I did not know Him, He had placed in me a desire to learn about Him. I shared my problem with a friend and she readily invited me to her Sunday school. It was within walking distance of my home. A whole new world was about to be introduced to me.

CHAPTER 2 – GOD CONFRONTS ME

"Then Jesus came to them and said, "All authority is given to me. Therefore go and make disciples of all nations, baptizing them in the name of the Father and of the Son and of the Holy Spirit, and teaching them to obey everything I have commanded you. And surely I am with you always, to the very end of the age."
-Matthew 28:18-20

Pleasant View, the small community in which we now lived, is outside Golden, Colorado. Rev. Paul Eiselstein, an American Sunday School Union Missionary, started the Sunday school there. Rev. Eiselstein was called "Uncle Paul" by everyone. He started over 103 Sunday schools in the state. He would gather a group of people together and eventually help them call a pastor to organize the Sunday school into a church. When I moved to Pleasant View, the church had been organized, and Rev. Bob Petersen was its pastor.

Pastor Bob was an accomplished musician. (He is the brother of the Christian composer, John Peterson.) He loved guitar music and played the steel guitar himself. When I began attending the church, he immediately asked if I could sing. As you know, music was very much a part of our home. We had a baby grand piano which both Dad and Mom played, and music was exciting to me. To Pastor Bob's delight, I could sing.

Since my mother and sisters started attending the church with me, Pastor Bob asked my mother if she, my sisters, and I would sing in Sunday school. We did. Immediately after the service he asked me to sing in the guitar band. He promised to teach me to play the ukulele. The group had a fifteen-minute radio broadcast every Sunday morning.

After some weeks of practice I became the soprano in a trio. I was nine; Linda, our alto, was eight; and Elaine, age ten, sang tenor an octave above the written tenor part. We became famous! Our harmony was perfect and we were indignant that people were so amazed that we sang so well. Now I realize it is very unusual for children of that age to sing harmony and I understand their amazement. Because of singing on our regular Sunday morning radio show, our trio was asked to sing in many churches around the Denver area.

So it was within this environment, with God working through wonderful people, that I saw the love of Christ and was compelled to come to Him.

One Sunday morning Pastor Bob preached about my need to accept Christ as my own personal Lord and Master. I needed to let Him know I was aware of the sin in my life, ask His forgiveness, and make Him Lord of my life.

My sins loomed up in front of me. I couldn't count how many pennies and nickels I had stolen from my dad. Many times I had sassed my mother. and my sisters—a great jealousy burned in my heart against them. I had been an only child for four years and then they had invaded my life. But I realized hatred had nailed Christ to the cross. So the conviction of the Holy Spirit surged up within me. I was embarrassed, ashamed, and I cried.

I rushed from the church after prayer, ran down Highway 40 to my own home, and into my room. Hidden under the covers of my bed with a flashlight and my Bible, I read again Romans 10:9-10 and with tears rolling down my cheeks I cried out to God for forgiveness and love. I needed His love for I often felt so lonely. Pastor Bob had told me Jesus loved me so much He had died in my place. Now that is real love! So into Jesus' hands I placed myself. I was now forgiven, loved, and starting the most exciting life a person could have. I fully understand and agree 100% with John 10:10. Life in Christ is more than abundant. It *is* life!

CHAPTER 3 – POINT OF NO RETURN

"Therefore go and make disciples . . . baptizing them."
- Matthew 28:19-20

Making a disciple of a nine-year-old can be difficult. On the other hand, at nine a child is easily molded. I enjoyed the prestige of singing on the radio, singing before groups of people, and being accepted by a group of new friends. I tried to play on the piano all the songs we sang at church and on the air. It became easier to pick each of them out. Of course, I played them all in the key of C because that involves no sharps or flats (the black keys.)

With all the practice at home and continual training from Pastor Bob, I was a good disciple in music. Then it happened. Sin and Satan seem to always get in the way of walking with the Lord. Just when people are growing, he attacks and seeks to destroy.

Pastor Bob and his wife were asked to leave the church. Some said that because Pastor and his wife had no children of their own, they tried to steal the affection of the children from the church. "After all," they said, "he continually runs off here and there in the guise of singing for other churches." As a child I understood little of the real reasons Pastor and his wife were asked to leave, but I felt the people were personally attacking me. It became difficult to trust anyone. I felt they were hard and unloving. I doubted my parent's love because I didn't understand them. I had found a faithful friend in Jesus, but the one who had taught me about Jesus was gone. How could I learn more about Jesus, the only true friend I had? I knew I had to have someone teach me, and these people in the church hardly acted as if they even knew the Lord! Pastor Bob knew Him. What could I do?"

That summer the church was without a pastor, so the congregation asked Uncle Paul to direct a vacation bible school. Little did I know at the time how much this man would come to mean to me. He brought teachers and we had a wonderful week. I remember trying to memorize the entire chapter of John 14. When Uncle Paul came back for our program, he told us about a camp he had started. This was to be the camp's second summer of activity. He was limiting it to children aged ten and up, but I wanted to go! I talked to him after the program and he asked me how old I was.

"Oh dear," I said, "I'm nine and three-fourths."

"But you have to be ten to come to camp."

"Oh, please! I was just born late. All my friends and classmates at school are ten, and I fit right in! I'll be ten in October."

"We . . . I guess we could sneak you in if your folks don't mind."

So in 1948 I attended my first year at Camp Id-Ra-Ha-Je, a Christian camp that was originally started and run by Uncle Paul. Id-Ra-Ha-Je is the first two letters of each of the words in the song, "I'd Rather Have Jesus." The teachings and attitude of the camp director and staff reflected the theme song; indeed they would rather have Jesus than anything else.

I had never had such a wonderful time in all of my life! We learned the Bible, ate together, slept together, sang together, had guided play (without the usual childish battles that are never settled), and experienced a whole new atmosphere of love that I have never before felt. This was where I wanted to live and stay. When we had to return home, I could hardly face it. I did not want to go. It meant going back to sisters I fought with, to Dad, whom I was afraid of, and to Mom, whom I felt loved me least! I was learning how much Jesus loved me, and it was so nice. I vowed that I'd come back to this place as often as possible.

Pleasant View Community Church called a new pastor. He was nice enough but legalistic. His wife was jolly and plump. She had a beautiful deep voice and sang often. They had children—boys! He seemed to be a loving pastor, but of course things changed. Our guitar band was dissolved, and we no longer sang at other churches.

Just as youth begins to develop a love and confidence in someone, it is often destroyed. Or is this true in the adult world also? Soon the people of the church asked the new pastor to leave. I pled with him not to. He did leave, but took with him the people who were encouraged by his ministry. I decided to go with Pastor Patterson, and we began meeting in a garage. The group grew, and soon there was a new little church going, and I found a new group of friends.

After a time, we decided to build a church building and stabilize the membership. That meant the church had to decide on its affiliation. A new family that delighted us all had recently begun coming. The husband, Rev. DeNeui, was a representative for the General Association of Regular Baptists. Although he was unable to be there often because of his extensive travels, he settled his family in the area. What a boost to the group! It was a family of nine. The three older children were already away from home--the older two in the service and a married daughter soon to leave for the mission field. But that still left three girls and a boy at home. They were warm, loving people, and because of our respect for them, we felt the Baptists must be okay too. So the new little church associated itself with the General Association of Regular Baptists to receive help and encouragement.

To be a member of a Baptist church, one must be baptized. I had been baptized and wanted to join, so I went to inform Pastor Patterson that I was now old enough to join.

"Well, yes, I think you may be old enough," he said. "You are thirteen now?"

"Yes, and I know a *lot* about the Bible," I told him.

"Most thirteen-year-olds do!" said Pastor Patterson as he chuckled.

"And I've been in your church since it began."

"Yes, I know. But there is one small problem. You need to be baptized."

"Baptized? Oh no, Pastor, I was baptized when I was six."

"Did you know Jesus as your best friend and Savior then?"

"No. I found out about Jesus when I was nine. In fact, you know when I was ten, and you had just come to our church. I talked with you to be sure I had received Jesus in my life."

"Yes, I do remember. You felt very guilty about your sin and asked His forgiveness. Your life has proven that you really want everyone to know you love Him. So, you are ready to be baptized."

"But . . . pastor . . . I was . . . or anyway . . . I was baptized in my dad's church with my two sisters when I was six, Laura was two and Marty wad just a baby."

"But did you know Jesus then?" He asked.

"Well no, I guess not," I answered. Do you mean baptism has to come *after* you know Jesus?"

"Yes, that's it. It is to show people that you love Jesus and want to follow Him."

"I really didn't even know Jesus at age six so what did my baptism do?"

"Nothing, unless of course, your parents committed themselves to telling you about Jesus."

"Well, not exactly. So I need to be baptized again. OK, I don't mind. Do you have the baptismal basin?"

"No," he chuckled. "But we do have a place we can go to be baptized."

"God wouldn't mind if you just used a common basin, would He?"

"I don't think that's what He wants us to use. I think a river would be better."

"A river? Do we need that much water?" I was surprised.

"Where was Jesus baptized?" He asked.

"Jesus baptized? Oh, yes. I *do* remember. He was at the Jordan River, and a dove came down and rested on Him when He came out of the water. Out of the water?" I asked.

"Yes, he came *out* of the water. He was in the Jordan River. The book of Romans tells us baptism shows that we are buried with Christ in baptism because we want to be dead to sin. Then we come back to life and are resurrected as He was. Then we are to follow and obey Jesus."

"So I need to go *under* the water?!"

"Yes, to picture burial."

"But you don't know how much I *hate* water! I can't swim, and I've *never* put my head *under* the water!"

"Well, maybe this will be your first step of faith—obeying Jesus by following Him in baptism and trusting that you won't drown," he assured me.

I did struggle with the water! And I'm sure there were chuckles from those who watched, but now they knew I meant business. Jesus was the Lord of my life, and I was following Him. And I'm sure I can say that fear was in the hearts of Uncle Paul, Pastor Patterson, Rev. DeNeui, and Mrs.

Edmonds, my Sunday School teacher, as they felt the responsibility to continue discipling me. To bring this unlovely, strong-willed, insecure, hot-headed teenager to a knowledge of God and into obedience would be a challenge. But God had only asked them to be faithful—not work miracles. He would take care of that part.

CHAPTER 4 – GOD'S UNDERSHEPHERDS

". . . and teaching them to obey everything I have commanded you."
- Matthew 28:20

Mrs. Edmonds had been teaching me each Sunday. But now that the church was growing, they needed teachers for the smaller children that were attending. When we learn something, the Lord wants us to pass it on.

What better way to learn the Bible than to teach small wiggly children who could care less? Of course I was given a book that explained how to teach, but creativity entered quickly when Joey asked questions that were not in the book. I loved it. I was sharing with others the things I had learned during four years at Id-Ra-Ha-Je, things Mrs. Edmonds had taught me, and I was loving kids who might have felt as little love as I had.

My musical gifts were also being developed. I had finally learned how to play in keys other than C. Our baby grand piano sat beside a beautiful picture window in the living room. Because I was in school all day and had to do homework and chores when I arrived home, I found the only time to practice was at night. Fortunately, Dad had built an addition onto the back of the house, and while the rest of the family watched television in the back room, I sat by the hour in the living room picking out songs. I put chords with them and found that I could play almost any song I could sing.

My favorite way to play was in the dark. Often while moonlight shone in the window onto the keys, I would play—trying to make the piano sound as beautiful and smooth as the moonlight. It was beginning to be real music.

I also began to play the trumpet since this was Dad's instrument. I joined the band at school. I picked up playing the trumpet quickly, and since I always liked a challenge, I tried to be the best player in my section. Even now, I laugh at myself when I remember one challenge I took on.

It must have been late summer because the carnival had come to town. A cousin and I decided to take in the sights and the cotton candy. We didn't have much money to spend like many teenage girls, but that was all right. We were just looking for an excuse to be together and notice the boys. But that night it was a woman I noticed. As we walked down the street observing the "Fattest Woman on Earth," the 50-cent-a-shot booths, and all the lights, I heard a trumpet playing. There were also the sounds of a piano and drum, but so what? When we sauntered by, I was shocked to see one woman produced all those sounds. She had a trumpet in her right hand, played to piano with her left hand, and a drum with her foot. I'm sure I stood there amazed for ten or fifteen minutes. It was settled. If she could do that for a cheap carnival, I could do it for the Lord. She had certainly attracted a large number of us common people.

I'm glad for that challenge because even today when substitute teaching or speaking in churches, I can entertain a group of unwieldy children and gain real admiration. (Even adults sit up and take notice!) It's easier to teach when a child thinks the teacher is unique. If the class has a piano, I take out my trumpet and play the two together. If there is no piano, I cart along my accordion and play the accordion and trumpet together. Most people have never seen this done and so it is a real attraction. I promise more music after the lessons are finished.

Being an energetic, active person, I quickly found there were too few things to do at the church. So I asked Uncle Paul if he knew of some things for me to do and groups for me to join. He had a program in the public schools called "Pioneers for Christ." There was a P.F.C. meeting during the lunch hour in the high school and a weekly meeting at Uncle Paul's house.

In the meetings at Uncle Paul's, he often took the position of an atheist or rebellious teenager and challenged us to convince him he should be a believer in the Lord. One ground rule was that only the Bible would convince him. It was amazing how much value we put in our own logic and words. We were reminded again and again that it is only the word of God that really convicts and changes hearts. So, although I was only in junior high school, I walked over to the high school at noon to be at P.F.C. Club meeting. Each week I was allowed to attend the evening club. My discipleship classes in knowing the word and becoming a leader had begun.

After my freshman year in high school, at age fourteen, I began working for Uncle Paul and Id-Ra-Ha-Je. His program consisted of many small vacation Bible schools all over the Colorado mountains and six weeks of camp. Each week of camp catered to a specific age group of children. By now we were building our own camp, and each year it was expanding to accommodate a larger number of campers.

My first assignment was an easy one. Each day, Gail Day, a young married lady, came to pick me up, and we went up Golden Gate Canyon to a little Sunday school there. I would teach the small children and Gail, the older ones. The vacation Bible school went all day, from 9:00 A.M. to 3:00 P.M. Since things went well that first week, the next week I was sent to a town much farther away and lived at the church while I taught vacation Bible school.

Week after week, two or three teachers were placed in a mountain town to live in a trailer, a church basement, a home with a receptive family, or a motel. There in a town hall, church, or garage, a vacation Bible school was held. Our resources were limited: lesson books for the children and a few crayons. Sometimes we had activities after club, but always, either on

Friday night or Sunday morning, the children would give a program for the parents.

"Welcome, ladies and gentlemen. Tonight we would like to sing a few songs, share a few verses, and let you see the crafts the children have made."

"Same song, second verse: a little bit louder and a little bit worse!"

Can you imagine doing that same program six times a summer? Using the same songs, same verses, same crafts? My very being cried out against such boredom. Jesus was God! He was alive, well, exciting, and drawing the crowds. How could we do any less? He had said Himself, "I tell you the truth, anyone who has faith in me will do what I have been doing. He will do even greater things than these, because I am going to the Father." John 14:12.

Actually, we did the "common" program only two times, not six. We decided every program had to be alive, unique, and full of creativity. The children needed to create their own situations to tell the Bible story they had studied. So Johnny became David. He wore a costume. In scene one the parents found Johnny out tending the sheep, and as he played his harp, the sheep spoke English and sang a song! The lion David killed was Joe—that youngster who was glib for his age but unable to remember a single verse. (Later, he also appeared as Goliath). When the program was over, the children knew the Bible story, realized they had learned a number of songs, and were proud because they were part of a production. But best of all, the parents were proud of their children because they had done well! Most of the parents had never seen their children act in any type play, so it was unique and exciting to find that their children could produce such dramas.

Never again would I do a "typical" program of recitation. Creativity stimulates thinking, reinforces learning, and is a whole lot more fun. In learning this practical lesson of creative, stimulating presentations, I was forming a part of my life that has continued to be one of my goals. That goal is to engage people in creative presentations causing them to long remember the lesson to be learned. I strive to teach by involving the student to express what they learn by way of dramas. I was by nature a strong-willed, active, creative person who used those traits for God in a positive way, instead of just building my own ego.

Uncle Paul, this little Jewish man of five feet, four inches, had decided to change his world. He *looked* for strong-willed kids like me. Then he challenged them to use their energies in a productive way. I'm sure he had fifty-sixty of us. How he ever kept us all straight with the wild program he ran, I'll never know. But each summer he held between sixty-ninety vacation Bible schools and had six weeks of camp. At each camp there were three to four hundred kids.

Uncle Paul considered this group of kids his disciples. As Jesus trained twelve to continue the work He did, so Uncle Paul wanted to train people to teach children and spread the Word of God. After sending each of us into the small villages of Colorado to teach vacation Bible schools, he then sent us to camp where there was close supervision. Uncle Paul allowed me to counsel the younger children. When the groups of campers were my age or older, my work was cleaning the outhouse. When that job was completed, I worked in the kitchen with Aunt Mary, the chief cook—and a stern one to boot! There I learned how to cook for one hundred campers, how to peel potatoes, including the intricacies of taking out each eye. I cried when I peeled onions and found out powered eggs are okay in cakes but not nearly as tasty scrambled. Government surplus butter, which we had a camp, was far superior to margarine, and I had a hard time eating margarine back at home.

What does a person learn cleaning a stinky out-houses? Sweeping out the chapel? Making rock-lined paths through the forest? Obedience and faithfulness. You learn to ask God for a good attitude so you don't fall into self-pity or discouragement. When the Pine-sol falls down the hole, you quickly realize anger doesn't bring it back. At best the little outhouse smells better! You learn that if you hold the hand of your friend, Jesus, you can feel His power in you and can begin to overcome the temper your father so ably taught you. *Occasionally*, a camper or fellow worker thanks you for your job well done, and you feel the love God talks about that Christians have for one another.

Uncle Paul believed that to really train a person means to be with them in life—living and working together in everyday activities—showing them what you know and how having a friend like Jesus makes a difference. Uncle Paul lived an example before us that we could follow. He reminded me of Saint Paul who said in I Corinthians 11:1, "Follow my example, as I follow the example of Christ." Truly Uncle Paul did follow Jesus, and we could follow him.

  It was during my first summer of working at Camp Id-Ra-Ha-Je, when I was fourteen, that I chose a life verse, Philippians 3:10 "I want to know Him . . ." I'd learn other parts of that verse later in life, but for the next four years, getting to know Jesus was my goal and priority. I spent every summer working in vacation Bible schools and at camp. I spent every Saturday night attending Youth for Christ in Phipp's Auditorium in Denver, Colorado, so I could hear what other people knew about Jesus. I spent every noon at P.F.C. Club in Golden High School. My goal was to know Jesus. I know I wrote notes in church just like every other teenager, but often the Holy Spirit got through, and I learned more about Christ. I'm still learning about Him, and I'm sure I'll only know Him fully when I fall into His arms in glory.

CHAPTER 5 – WHAT HAS GOD GIVEN?

*"We have different gifts, according
to the grace given us."*
- Romans 12:6

    Often insecurity brings determination to prove self-worth. Teenagers constantly struggle to accept themselves. I was not an exception. Because of my home life, I had *very* strong feelings of insecurity. I was sure my parents were not interested in me, my sisters and I were in constant competition and battles, and I could count the dates I had as a high school student on one hand. I now realize that my bossy, outgoing behavior was an attempt to prove my self-worth. When insecurity raises its head, it is ugly. It often shows itself by being fearful and by retreating into a corner of self-rejection. But more often it shows itself by being bold and putting others down. Because I was so insecure, I constantly tried to prove to my peers that I was worth something, that I could do some very outstanding things. But amidst my struggle to establish self-worth, God was at work. He used my wrong efforts to teach me from where I had gotten the gifts and talents I had and to teach me about His love.

    Music had become a natural way for me to build self. I was playing the piano rather well, was in the high school's special group of nine girls who sang three and four-part harmony songs, and was also in the school band. For two years I had been third chair in the trumpet section. Finally, in my senior year, I was due to be promoted to first chair. The two boys ahead of me were graduating. But to my dismay, I learned that a freshman, who had had five years of private lessons and was very good, was coming to Golden High School.

    Mr. Bevill was our band teacher. One day I approached him about this very important challenge that I found I was facing.

    "Mr. Bevill, isn't there something I can do over the summer to improve myself and keep the first chair?"

    "Well, Ivy," he said, "perhaps, but I've noticed after each concert your lip is *really* marked. I think you may be playing your trumpet the wrong way. If you want the full effect of playing, you'll have to change your embouchure."

"And what exactly does that mean?"

"At present you are using only your upper lip. You need to develop the lower lip as well, so there is equal pressure giving you a fuller range of sound. It shouldn't be too hard and in three months, if you practice daily, you can change over and be able to keep your chair."

Needless to say, I never expected to have to re-learn my whole method of playing, but I was determined. No freshman was going to outplay me!

So the summer began. During the first six weeks, I lived each week in a different community holding vacation Bible school from 9:00 A.M. to 3:00 P.M. And then I practiced my trumpet for an hour in the afternoon. Readjusting my method was difficult. I had to over-use my lower lip to begin developing it, giving a rest to the top lip to balance out the pressure. I certainly sounded like a beginner.

The third week of the summer I taught in Empire, Colorado. My fellow teacher, June, was a student from Moody Bible Institute and was learning to play the accordion. We were a noisy but determined pair as we practiced each afternoon. After three days in Empire, the determination was gone, and I was about to give up.

"June, it's hopeless. I played this horn *well* before, but now I sound like I'm just starting! That band director must want to ruin my chances."

"Oh Ivy, I'm sure that's not true. And you sound a little better today."

I couldn't help noticing her turned head and hidden chuckle. "I don't believe it. I'm going to skip this. I think he was wrong, and I'm just going to play like I did before."

Well, with that decision I forsook the new method to return to just playing for enjoyment. Much to my dismay, that ability was also gone. The overworked muscles in my upper lip had relaxed so that they refused to play alone as before.

The next day I tried again and found I could no longer play. June was feeling defeated about her accordion, and I'll never forget the results: two teachers, kneeling side by side at our little bed in the trailer, crying our eyes out. But June did have a thought. "God is the one who gave us the desire to play, and the talent. Maybe we haven't been using it for Him." Now that was a new thought, and guilt flooded my mind. True, I wanted to use my trumpet to show Golden High School that I, a girl, was its top trumpeter. I wanted to beat out a freshman. I wanted to be known, to have the solos at concerts, and represent our school at contests. Realizing that I was using the gift God had given me for myself, I asked forgiveness and gave it back to Him.

"Lord, thank you for giving me the desire and abilities to play. I want to give that talent back to you, to use it to play for you, and let people know that you are the giver of all perfect gifts.

No, a miracle did not take place. I really don't believe much in modern-day miracles except for spiritual ones. I was not able to play correctly after my confession and prayer. But I knew now my motives were right. I'd learn to play again for God, and it probably would take the full three-month, as Mr. Bevill had said, before it sounded good.

The very next week, and after only three days of further practice, I was taken to Indian Hills, Colorado, where I had taught before. The children there knew me. The previous summer I had entertained them often with my piano/trumpet duet. Yes, you read right. Since I knew how to play both instruments, I had developed the skill of playing the piano with my left hand and holding the trumpet with my right hand and thus was able to play both instruments at the same time.

"Ivy, Ivy! Do it again! There are new kids here this year, and they want to see you do it!"

What should I do? For two days I put them off. All kinds of excuses came up, especially the one that I just couldn't play. I was learning a new method; my lips weren't in shape yet, and so on. But the pressure was on. I finally decided to try. Then I would no longer have to make excuses because they would hear for themselves that I couldn't play.

Before I went to the piano; in fact, while I stood behind it putting my mouthpiece into place, I prayed, "Lord, this trumpet is yours. You and I both know I can't play very well yet, so please prepare the kids for the disappointment."

I took my seat at the piano, laid the trumpet across my lap and began the introduction to "Onward Christian Soldiers." Up came the trumpet and out came the sound. God had not needed to prepare the children for disappointment but me for a shock. The sound was clear-- more precise than ever in my life. The high notes flowed out like the sounds of the professionals from the Denver Symphony Orchestra. The song finished, and tears flooded my eyes. I could not believe it. The kids ran to the piano, hugging and thanking me as they went home for the day.

    In the quiet of the room, I picked up my trumpet and said, "God, it was you. It couldn't have been me. Please, let me try again without your help." Sure enough, it wasn't exactly the same sound made by a squealing sow, but it was definitely that of a beginning trumpeter.

    Perhaps now I did believe in an occasional miracle, but I continued to practice throughout the summer. When school began in September, I met my rival, John. He beat me the first month, but as I improved I challenged him and won the first chair. The year was like a seesaw—he was first chair awhile, and then I was. But my attitude had changed. The horn belonged to God. I played it for Him.

    My best friend in band saw that change. She saw John and I were friends. Because we were both Christians, we complimented and encouraged each other rather than being in competition. We shared the solos and enjoyed playing together.

    "Ivy, what has changed you?" my friend Bonnie asked. "You told me last year you'd never let John be ahead of you, but now when he is, you don't even mind. I wish I had that kind of attitude."

    "Bonnie, it isn't a natural one to me. I realized God gave me the talent to play my trumpet to begin with, so this summer I decided to play it for Him. Last year I was only interested in people seeing how good I was. Well, now I don't care. I want to play well for the Lord, but my desire is to please Him, not me." Because of that talk, Bonnie began to attend Pioneers For Christ with me and soon had the desire to learn more about following the Lord and living for Him.

CHAPTER 6 - CAN A SCHOOL HELP?

"When my father and mother forsake me . . . then the Lord will take me up."
- Psalm 27:10

After living in Colorado all of my life and attending the only grade school and high school in Golden, Colorado, I chose to go to Westmont College in Santa Barbara, California. Here God continued to lead me. The lessons I had to learn were more intense; much more difficult and rewarding—powerful, you could say.

Because my parents were not Christians and had no money to help me attend college, they were not in favor of my going. But being a stubborn and strong-willed adolescent, I disobeyed and went. So began four years of growth and real struggles.

A few weeks before I left for Westmont, I overheard my sister and mother talking in the kitchen.

"You just wait! She will get to that school and immediately ask for money! Well, we aren't going to send her any!" said my mother, indignantly.

I decided then that I would never ask my folks for money. God was able to care for me, and it was to Him that I would go to. Indeed, that was the way it turned out. However, in retrospect, I think I should have tried to obey my parents. I did go back after my junior year at Westmont and ask their forgiveness. I praise God I did. When you keep hurt and anger in your heart and never resolve them, you can experience continual guilt. Asking both the person and God for forgiveness can only rectify it.

When it was time to leave for school, I went to tell the family goodbye. My mother was crying. My sisters said goodbye and ran off. My dad came out of the house:

"If you *do* go, don't ever come back!"

He stormed back into the house and Mom followed him.

Just before leaving Colorado in September to start school, I had renewed an old friendship with Jim, one of the older brothers of my best friend, Dorothy. He was attending Biola—Bible Institute of Los Angeles. Since Westmont was also in Southern California, we traveled together in his car. Could this be my future husband? We did talk about it and became engaged on that trip. It only added confusion to my life since Biola was ninety miles south of Westmont. We were both full-time students and had little time to be together. We corresponded, but that took time, which should have been spent in study. After about two months, we both realized our relationship was cooling; the effort of maintaining it was too taxing, and maybe we had grabbed at security in each other rather than God, so we broke the engagement. We continued to be friends but soon even our friendship faded.

I found college classes very difficult and had to study for the first time in my life. I met with my first academic failure. The jobs didn't roll in, and I had no money whatsoever! I was definitely struggling. God brought a very special couple into my life at that time.

I noticed that one of the churches in town needed an attendant for the nursery on Sunday evenings, and it was a paying job. I jumped at the chance of earning some money—besides I liked kids and had lots of experience of working with them. In the nursery that night I met Mrs. Niesen. She was a member of the church and was in charge of the cafeteria at Westmont. That evening we became very good friends. I felt as if I had found a real mother. I told her of my problems, and she asked me to report to the cafeteria the next day. She showed me the vegetable-shed and how to work the potato peeler. She also gave me a few hints on preparing vegetables for the three hundred students at the school. Since I had had experience from camp, the job was easy, and I was hired on the spot. I could work any hours of the day I had free, and so I was able to have a job right at the school and continue my classes as required.

Mr. and Mrs. Niesen became like parents to me, and I spent time in their home seeking the counsel and love I needed.

One of my great needs in life seems to be "beholding the creation of God." I had grown up in Colorado with its majestic mountains, snow-covered peaks, ice-cold streams, and indeed, the rocks. I could sit beside a stream for hours listening to the water splashing over the rocks and gazing at the fascinating blue, yellow, white, and occasional "Indian paintbrush" flowers. In winter the soft floating snowflakes falling between the pines on a moonlit night enthralled me for hours. I still find my thoughts captured by the memory of the beauties there.

But California had new beauties and implanted new memories. Listening to the waves of the great Pacific Ocean hitting the beach also bewitched me. The rain falling among the eucalyptus trees on a wet winter day brought tantalizing smells. God continues to grasp my attention with His great creativity.

One evening at Westmont I was sitting on the porch of Stone Cottage under a full moon, looking out over the garden of palm trees and shrubs, smelling the eucalyptus that lined Montecito Street. The beauty should have been gripping my heart, but instead tears were flowing. I was homesick!

It was a mystery to me how I could be homesick. I was living in a beautiful setting, among wonderful Christian friends, and doing what I had always dreamed of doing; nevertheless, I was homesick for a family that preferred I didn't return, one that fought a good deal of the time, one I had never missed before. Strange feelings. Sick inside feelings. Feelings I couldn't explain, understand, or chase away. The ache, the desperation, I realized for the first time how much I did love that family God had given me. Most often we forget the bad things that happen to us and remember the good. I forgot a fishing trip when my father's anger caused him to break his fishing pole and throw it into the river and recalled the times of joy when he caught his limit. I forgot the tears in Mom's eyes when she and Dad fought and remembered happy times such as eating popcorn around the TV.

But these terrible feelings were good reason to cling to my Savior. "When my father and mother forsake me, then the Lord will take me up," Psalm 27:10. God was calling me to depend completely on Him. He was my sole provider and comfort. He would meet my every need and teach me His love. In the moonlight I knelt before God and called to Him for comfort, for peace. And with that cry, His love flooded me, assuring me again of His peace and presence.

It was nearing Christmas, and I was generally confused and lonely. The very next day I received a letter from Mom saying Dad could hardly wait until I came home for Christmas. My heart leaped for joy! So my dad's having told me, "Don't come back here if you go to that college" was just a threat to try to keep me at home. They *did* still want me to be a part of the family; I had not lost them. Perhaps during this vacation I could share the love of God more effectively with Dad. It seemed that God was making a way for me to be reconciled with my family.

The following days were happier. I even talked to Dutch, one of my dear friends at Westmont, about how I could help the kids from Westmont who were going to Hawaii.

"Say, Ivy, we sure would like for you to join the outreach team that is going to Hawaii. Two more kids dropped out, so we'd have room on the team for you."

"Now, Dutch," I responded, "You know my financial situation. My folks couldn't help at all. I'm in debt to the school now, and I'd like to come back next year. You have a good team. I will promise to pray. Do you have anything else I could do?"

"Well, we are going to need plenty of Bibles. Do you know where we could get some used ones?"

"Are you kidding? We have millions of them at camp. You know how kids are. When 4,000 kids come to camp each year, lots of them forget their Bibles. We try to get them back to the kids, but when we fail, we store them up to give away to those who didn't have them. I bet Uncle Paul would let me have some of those."

"Great! That would be a big help."

By Christmas that first year, many of my frustrations were solved. I realized my parents did love me, and I was to spend Christmas again in beautiful snowy Colorado. Mrs. Nieson had helped me get a good job, and now I had a job to do for the Lord. I would fill boxes with Bible to bring back for the Lei O'Limas, the team of students planning to spend the following summer in Hawaii working in the churches on the Island of Maui.

That first Christmas home after making the break to go to college was beautiful! It was good to be together as a family again. I know my sisters thought I was an extra big show off, and we did have our fights, but it seemed they had missed me a bit. I spent a week at camp, our winter retreat, and sure enough, Uncle Paul gave me 176 Bibles. Bibles were stuffed into every nook and cranny of the car I rode back in, but the students I rode with accepted their discomfort with good humor; they understood that it was for a worthy cause.

January 1957, progressed much better. I began to feel as if I belonged at Westmont and the homesickness left me. Although I failed "Man and Civilization," I learned how to study and the second semester, I passed. I found myself praying for the Lei O'Limas often and even attending some of their meetings so I could pray more effectively. Soon I found I had a desire to join them. But that was impossible! It was true I now had jobs that were more lucrative than working in the vegetable shed at the school, but I did not have enough to pay school bills and the $300 extra which I would need to go to Hawaii.

About the time I was struggling with the desire to go, the church job ended, and one of my other jobs stopped. So, second semester I was faced with a school bill and little money. One day when I went to my post box (a much-visited place) I found a letter from the business office.

"Dear Miss Owens," it read. "You have an outstanding bill of $240. This bill must be paid tomorrow, March 27th, or you will not be able to continue your schooling at Westmont."

$240 in one day? How? Oh help! I would not get paid for any of my jobs until the next week. Would I borrow the money? But from whom? And how could I ever pay it back? I was in college by faith, so by faith I prayed.

"Lord, if you want me to stay here, you will have to provide a miracle. I have no money and have no idea where it will come from. If you want me to go home, I am willing, but I don't even have money for the bus fare."

The next day I again went to the post box. There were three letters—one from the business office and two from school friends in Colorado. I opened the two letters from friends first. One was from Gary Risdon, who was a senior at Golden High. Gary was a fellow Pioneer for Christ member and was also from a non-Christian home.

"Dear Ivy," he began. "I have a part-time job after school and know it's tough to be on your own at college. Just thought you might be able to use this $10 to help out." The rest of the news he shared was about friends and what he was up to.

Then I opened letter number two. It was from Leslie Korthuis, a friend from school and camp who had graduated the year before me.

"Hey, Ivy. I bet you forgot, but last summer you loaned me $20. I never paid you back. So here it is with interest. Hope it helps out with your expenses." Enclosed were two $20 bills.

Well, the Lord had sent the money for a bus ticket home. OK, if that were what I was to do, I'd do it. As I slowly climbed the steps up to the business office to tell them I could not pay the bill so I'd be checking out, I tore open their letter. What a shock!

"Dear Miss Owens, We are happy to inform you that an anonymous donor from Pasadena, California, has applied $200 to your bill."

I knew no one in Pasadena. Who could it be? Why? How could it happen? Well, only God knows, but it was with great joy that I continued to that office to pay the additional $40 and tucked the $10 in my purse to give to the Lord on Sunday.

How about Hawaii? I still owed the school for the second half of the semester and of course had none of the $300 needed to go with the team. The struggle continued, but finally I decided to try to go. I determined to work extra hard for the rest of the school year and the two weeks between the end of school and our leaving for Hawaii, I'd get a full-time job at school. I had real peace about the decision to join the team although I was very unsure of how God would raise the money. I told the team I felt God wanted me to join them. I began singing with them and planning to go.

A few days later I saw a notice on the school bulletin board. "P.E. teacher wanted, Montecito School for Girls." A telephone number was given so I called. I loved to teach P.E. classes. P.E. was my minor at Westmont and the Montecito School was close by. I got the job.

Every Tuesday and Thursday afternoon I conducted PE. Classes for about twelve girls aged nine to twelve. Not only was it fun, but they also became dear little friends. I told them about my plans to go to Hawaii, and they found out I had taken the job to raise the money to go. As the school year neared its end, they also learned I feared I would not be able to raise *enough* money to go. On the last day of school they had a surprise farewell party for me. They handed me a box about five inches square. It was the heaviest box I had ever held. Opening it, I found it full of quarters, dimes, nickels and pennies! These girls had raided their piggy banks and collected about $75 in change. A lot of money for 1957! Needless to say I was overwhelmed. This was one of many steps, which led to the miracle of my going to Hawaii on Lei O'Lima team number one, June to August. 1957.

Why was God so faithful to me? Because He *is* faithful. "Make disciples . . . teaching them to obey everything . . . and surely I will be with you always . . . " Matthew 28:20. "And my God will meet all your needs according to His glorious riches in Christ Jesus." Philippians 4:19. "The one who calls you is faithful and He will do it." I Thessalonians 5:24.

I believe when we obey the commands God gives us, He honors us. I had been taught my last summer at Camp Id-Ra-Ha-Je that it is good to tithe. In fact, for weeks Malachi 3:10 had haunted me. I knew I would need about $135 a month for my expenses at Westmont. I should therefore give at least $13 a month to Him. I knew I'd want to give to a church and perhaps Youth for Christ, but I needed to bind myself to part of that tithe. We always can stand more firmly if we are accountable to someone. So having met Evelyn Kness, an excellent teacher and friend at Id-Ra-Ha-Je, I pledged $10 a month to her support. She was a missionary to the Dominican Republic. Faithfully, each month, I had taken $10 from the money I received at work and sent it to her.

I am so thankful I learned the blessing of giving. Jesus was right when He said, "It is more blessed to give than to receive." Acts 20:35. And now I also experienced the promise in Malachi " . . . and see if I will not throw open the floodgates of heaven and pour out so much blessing that you will not have room enough for it."

CHAPTER 7 – HAWAII — A STEPPING STONE

*"Go into all the world and preach
the good news to all creation."*
-Mark 16:15

    I had been told Hawaii was a nature lover's heaven, and I was a true nature lover. I could hardly wait to visit this special garden of God's. In addition, I'd never been on a plane before, so my emotions, anticipations, and expectations ran rampant when, along with twenty-three others, I boarded that United Airlines flight bound for Honolulu. I was not to be disappointed; things became more exciting and exhilarating as the trip continued.

    When we disembarked, Christians in Honolulu who adorned our necks with seven lei's apiece greeted us. I have never seen to many flowers with such tantalizing scents! And the scenery, the balmy temperature, the swaying palm trees and the warm sand! Yep, it *was* heaven! Thus began my three-month stay in the islands of Hawaii.

    We spent one week in Honolulu ministering with Youth for Christ, seeing the annual celebration of national Hawaiians (the parade, King Kamehameha, the traditional dancing and singing), and finally celebrating at an authentic luau with roasted pig and all the trimmings.

    Then we moved to Maui, our center of ministry. Here we experienced a big change! In Honolulu we had lived in ultra-modern hotels. Maui was much more rural and run down. The house we rented was across the street from a sugar factory. Have you ever lived close to a sugar factory? Well . . . the rent was cheap, the house was big, and it housed most of our twenty-four members. It had a kitchen and a bit of furniture, but we soon learned why. We all learned to drop *everything* when the factory whistle blew to announce quitting time. If we hadn't we would all be deaf today. The steady noisy grinding of the machinery eventually became almost bearable, but we never did stop praying that if the wind changed and blew in our direction, it would *quickly* change back again! The smell of sugar processing is *not* sweet!

The termites had begun doing "a job" on the house and furniture. However, in the three months we lost only one sofa. One day, even with the ropes we had tied around it to hold the sofa together, the bottom broke out and when we tried to pick it up, we found the termites had finished it all. We carried it out in pieces.

Because of my experience at Id-Ra-Ha-Je and in the kitchen at Westmont, I was asked to be in charge of all the meals. I was to plan and organize them. I could assign people to help with the buying and cooking. Organizing the food and preparation of it became my main responsibility for the summer. As the team's ministry began, I soon learned to plan easy breakfasts, provided for those who had to take packed lunches, and suppers for more than the twenty-four team members. One of the customs of Hawaii was to have guests, and rarely a night went by that we didn't have at least two to twenty extra guests. We always had enough pineapple! Yum!

Living in a different culture brought lots of new excitement and learning. Because I was working with Japanese people, my first feat was to learn to eat with chopsticks. It took quite a few lessons, but I soon could keep up with the best of them. I still found it awkward to put the rice bowl to my mouth and shovel it in! Somehow my culture had so ingrained in me that this was not right, that I never could easily do it. I also struggled with drinking the soup from the bowl.

A Japanese bath was also very different! You would go into the bathhouse and dip water from the upright tub onto your skin. Then you would soap down and again dip the water over your body to wash away the soap. When you were clean, you would climb into the "furo" an upright tub, sit on a small chair in the water and sink down to your chin. The fire under the tub would then be built up and you soaked until the water became so hot you had to jump out!

Japanese people are so, so, so, polite! Answers to questions must never offend. They must *never* make you look like you do not know something. They must always "save face." That means they can never do anything that would make the other person look foolish or to appear to not know the answer to a question. In other words, you never say to a Japanese person, "Is the Congregational Church down this street?" For the answer is always, "Oh, yes. Just ahead." When in fact, it is the other way! If they were to say, "No, the church is the other way," they feel they would be making you look like you were wrong. We soon learned how to ask questions!

With time, I learned a bit of the Japanese culture. Three of our team were assigned to a Congregational Japanese Church. We were to work with the pastor and set up youth and children's programs for the summer. I worked with the children while Kilani, our Hawaiian team director and Carol, worked with the youth. Our first assignment was for Sunday school. We met with the pastor in the side room to pray and discuss what we would do. It was decided that pastor would introduce us, and I would tell an opening story. Then the children and adults would be dismissed to their classes, which we would visit. Kilani would be speaking in the morning worship.

The butterflies would not settle in my stomach. But I prayed and asked God what story I should tell. I was convinced I was to tell my best—"Big Jim." With that settled, I told the pastor what I would be teaching and settled back to wait for the time to come.

When we entered the sanctuary, I was shocked! In the very back row of the church sat two very elderly men and one elderly woman. There was absolutely no one else in the room!

"Lord, am I to tell my very best story to three people?"

"Yes."

`   "But Lord, wouldn't it be best to save it for a day when there would be more children here? If I tell it now . . . well, it seems it will be wasted!"

"No, it won't be wasted. You are to tell 'Big Jim.'"

"But Lord!"

Yet for the life of me, I was so shaken that I couldn't even remember another story. And before I could think about it any more, the pastor announced my coming to tell the story of "Big Jim."

I respond best when I am communicating with children! To communicate with empty seats and three elderly people, needless to say, it took all the strength I had to put my best into that story and tell it the way I knew God would want me to tell it.

At the end, Kilani, the pastor, Carol and the three old people clapped. Then the pastor dismissed the group to their classes.

Amazing! This just cannot be! What happened next was something I can still remember clearly. From behind the tall-backed benches stood over sixty children! They rushed from their seats to the class not daring to look at that white person who had just enthralled them. Yes, they were that shy!

In the following weeks, on a Sunday morning, eyes would occasionally peek up over the back of the benches but quickly disappear if I looked their way; however, with time, they sat up and smiled. They found that this strange white person loved them, played with them, and soon was taking them on outings to play baseball or go to the beach.

Another time I remember the Lord and I had a deep discussion about what lessons I was to teach in the two-days-a-week Bible class. I knew very quickly that most of these children did not know the Lord. The pastor preached literally from the *Readers Digest* and the teachers gave them stories from school readers. They did have the Old Testament reading and the New Testament reading but no commentary was made about either of the Bible readings.

"Lord, these children need to learn about salvation and their need to receive you."

"I want you to teach Ephesians 6."

"They don't even know why they need armor! They aren't even in the army yet!"

"I said Ephesians 6."

"Lord, why?"

"Will you obey?"

"OK, but it doesn't make sense to me!"

So for the next eight weeks we talked about the battle against Satan and the armor we were to put on. We made the belt of truth and the breastplate of righteousness. The cardboard breastplate proved a strong cover for the cardboard swords we made later. The rest of the armor took shape and I did my best to explain why each part of the armor was necessary. I taught them a song about it all, and at the end of the study, presented a lovely program; the children arrayed in their armor, delivered explanations and songs. The presentation was flawless, what I did not expect is what happened after the program.

After the drama, the church had prepared a farewell party for the three of us who had worked at the church. Around the dessert table, children continued to come up to me with tears in their eyes.

"Aunt Ivy. I understand now why I need the armor. I want to be in God's army. How can I do that? You are leaving, and I really must know!"

Thus went the entire evening. One by one the children came until almost every participant had accepted Christ as Savior. Now I understood why God had me teach the armor. They now had something to hang onto in their new Christian lives. God knew they were so shy that they would not be bold enough to follow Christ at the beginning. So, in a way, we did put the cart before the horse. We taught them how to walk the Christian life before they actually needed to know, but when they all came to Him the day before we left, they had the knowledge of how to grow. So, once again, I learned to obey God.

I realize now that the last part of the great commission says, "teaching them to obey everything I have commanded you." I was indeed learning to obey and realizing that it really is best since He knows the end of things!

I had one big heartbreak that summer. We realized from the beginning that the pastor was not a born-again person. He preached from the *Readers Digest* and seldom had any Biblical references at all. We began to pray for him and seek opportunities to share Christ with him. Many times during the summer, Kilani was able to share his testimony of how he had left Hawaii, gone to the mainland to study and there was introduced to Jesus. He had come back to tell his people about the Lord. Wouldn't pastor be interested? Although we knew he was very interested and listened intently, there was no decision made. Finally one day, the three of us had lunch with him. Time was short as we were to leave for the mainland in just one week so we pressed the pastor for a decision.

Pastor said, "Yes, I do understand that I need forgiveness of sin. I know that God loves me and that I really do need to accept Jesus as my Savior. I really believe what you are saying and would like to, but I can't."

"But why, Pastor? Your whole church needs to know the truth. If you understand you need His salvation, and want to, why can't you?"

"If I receive Jesus and begin preaching the Bible, I will lose my job."

"Impossible! How can that be?"

"Because we are told what to preach. When we do not follow what our leaders tell us to preach, we are asked to resign."

"Oh, Pastor. Please! Don't you realize that even to lose your job would be better than to lose eternal life!"

"I am sorry, but I want my job."

"That day all four of us cried, Kilani, Carol, the pastor and I. He really wanted to receive Jesus, but he loved his job more than the Savior. I learned that obedience to God may cost us everything, but it will be worth it in the long run.

I cannot end this part of my book without sharing one more step in my reconciliation with my family.

The team had decided to take the boat back to America. In those days, the cost of the boat trip was a bit less expensive than the airplane ride. We boarded a President Lines ship for the five-day trip back to the mainland.

When we came into port at San Francisco, my parents and sisters were waiting to meet me. Dad shared with me in a very faulty way that he really was proud of me. He had no friends whose daughter had gone to college and then traveled abroad! He seemed to be accepting the fact that I was determined to continue my education. He had also decided it was a bit of prestige for him to have a daughter In college and for her to become a world traveler.

We had a delightful time visiting the dock in San Francisco. I did have a bit of a problem walking straight down the sidewalk, and my sisters teased me a lot about being drunk. I tried to explain that after having to use sea legs for five days, it was not my fault that I couldn't walk straight! They continued to tease and imitate my walk! That night when I fell out of bed due to a swaying sensation, they really did tease me! By late morning the next day, I was a landlubber again!

My family and I drove to Westmont in Santa Barbara, and I was thrilled that I could share that part of my life with them. I knew I had a long way to go for reconciliation with my sisters. To them I appeared proud and seemed to be trying to show off. I still had a lot to learn.

PART II

"GET SET . . ."

CHAPTER 8 – WEAKNESS TO BECOME STRONG

"That is why, for Christ's sake, I delight in weakness."
-2 Corinthians 12:10

I was at the mark. I knew the Savior and had taken a firm stand for Him. He had let me serve in small ways—in Colorado and Hawaii, and I had learned some things about missions. But now I must get set. I must hone the essentials of being a Christian and make them useable. Paul had learned that by tough tests, we could become strong. God was now leading me through the tough test to enable me to endure in Uganda. So through weakness, I began the journey towards strength.

The sophomore year of college is supposed to be the best. You know many people and have many friends. You are not far enough along to wonder what in the world you will do after you graduate, and so the responsibilities of life aren't really a burden yet. I think this may have been particularly true in my life.

Alumni week was a special event and we went into the activities and events as if we were not in school at all and had no studies whatsoever. I was in the choir and had a great time singing under the leadership of Dr. John Hubbard. Every concert and practice, I majored in "funning." That word was to become a keyword in my vocabulary and life.

I was now living in Emerson Hall in the large room on the top floor. There were six of us in that room. Looking for daring and exciting things to do each weekend became our ultimate goal. Rules? We weren't sure why the school had them or if we should obey them. We were to be back in our room by midnight on Fridays and 11:00 P.M. on Saturdays. Just as a way of disobedience, we quickly learned how to climb out the window and slide down the drainpipe. This way we could leave the hall any time we chose and not be detected. The problem came with reentering the building.

All the "funning" and activities was a cover-up for the deep hurt and doubt I was experiencing. For the first time in my life, I was questioning God. How did I really know He existed? He had done many miracles in my life, but were they just coincident? I still felt very insecure and was continually trying to excel so others would notice me and see how great I was. But Westmont was not exactly the place for a Colorado hick to prove good.

Most of the students at Westmont were from wealthy families and were being financed by their parents. Everything they said and did was stylish and they vied for popularity and prominence. I was working full time and still had no extra money for anything, so I could not hope to compete with them.

I remember saving for about six months to buy a black sweater that I had seen in one of the shops downtown. I should have put the money toward my school costs but didn't. Finally, I had the $10 it cost and bought it! After I got it, I realized I had no skirt to go with it, it was not the right color for me, it was a bit too big, and my roommates said it just wasn't my style.

Another issue was that I had no boyfriends. One evening in the library, a young man came and sat beside me. He began talking quietly. Finally, he asked if I would like to go for a walk in the garden. I was so thrilled I almost didn't have the voice to respond. As we entered the garden I tried to be casual and friendly. After a couple of minutes he said, "Ivy, I just wanted to tell you that your clothes are terrible. They are all out of style, and you look like a country bum. I suggest you get your act together and dress in style."

With that, he left me standing alone in the garden. My mom had made all my clothes. They were all from high school days, but they were all I had. I received not one penny from my folks, and Westmont is not the most inexpensive Christian school in America. What was I to do?

Well, I didn't choose correctly. I began to doubt God. I asked myself, "How can I really believe all this stuff anyway?"

I'm not sure how it came about, but one day as I talked to one of the male students at Westmont; I found that he too doubted God. In fact, he didn't even believe there was a god—a real atheist! At Westmont? How could that be? In further conversation I found out that his mother had wanted him to attend Westmont so much that she had forced him to apply and actually lie about his belief in Christ.

At first I took Carl on as a challenge. I thought I could prove to him that there was a God, one that loved him and wanted to walk with him. But in our many discussions that followed, he began to make *me* doubt. Afternoons spent in deep conversations, we began to care about each other in a romantic way. He was extremely lonely and had no friends. I was looking for a boyfriend and he was beginning to be interested in me. Our relationship became secretive, and he began to hold and kiss me. I had little to remind me it was wrong. I was no longer reading my Bible. I seldom prayed; in fact, I didn't pray for over a month. His arguments became more and more convincing, and I was starved for love.

At Thanksgiving I had no place to go, so he invited me to go on the train with him to his home. His dad worked for the railroad, so he could get me a free ticket. His mother was thrilled to see that we were friends and begged me to try to get him to give his life to Christ. I assured her that I would do my best. But in reality I was coming closer and closer to where Carl was!

Our relationship was becoming more and more intimate. I really believed it was love. I felt I just had to spend the last hour before the Easter choir tour with Carl. After all, we would be apart for a whole week. We went for a walk into the beautiful hills of Santa Barbara. We sat on the ground and looked down at the lovely sights below: the blue Pacific spread in the distance; and almost tropical scene lay between the water and us—a very romantic setting. Soon Carl began to kiss me. He took me into his arms, and we lay back in the bushes. It was intense. Suddenly, I thought of the time. We had to run back to school so I could catch the choir bus leaving on tour.

After our concert the first night, we went to our host's home. While bathing I saw a small red spot on my leg. It itched a bit, and I scratched it. The next day I had more spots but thought nothing about it. The second night, in San Francisco, during the concert, I felt sick and hot. At the interlude I looked at my arms under the robe. I was covered with red, oozing spots. I was sure there were many more under my nylons. I couldn't tell anyone. I really didn't know what was wrong.

Later I was told that I passed out just after the last song, could not be revived, so our director, whose sister was in the audience, and some fellow students carried me to his sister's car. She took me to her home and upon examinations found that except for my face, my entire body was covered with poison oak! The next morning they called in a doctor, and he forced medicine into me to try to help, but the poison was also in the bloodstream, and I was pretty much unconscious for two days! That case of poison oak lasted eight weeks! I never told anyone how I had gotten it. But the guilt was there. In the quiet of my heart I knew that I had been rolling around in poison oak with Carl! I was so guilty that I cried, and finally I realized that God was calling me back. I could be forgiven and was! Never had God been so real to me as then. I understood how very, very sinful I was, how stupid, how unworthy, but God forgave! Thus began my breaking up with Carl and my walk back to the Lord. I praise God that our relationship ended when it did, or I'm sure there would have been sexual involvement and perhaps the ruination of my life.

****

With my spiritual life straightening, I was once again confronted with the prospect of going to Hawaii for a second year. Again there would have to be miracles to get me there, but God in His mercy began to supply and bless. The team was so excited. We had twenty-two people going but only five of us were repeats. The five of us would be able to orient the new people and be a stabilizing element to the team. Come June I was bound for Hawaii, a land and people I had learned to love!

This time I would meet friends from the year before, help them grow, and just be in that beautiful climate I had grown to desire! It was nothing like Colorado or California; it had a unique beauty. Tropical. All the flowers were bigger and brighter. The butterflies were so brilliant and delightful that you didn't have the heart to kill and collect them. The colorful birds turned everyone into "bird watchers." Everything was green! Plants were luscious and waterfalls so sparkling that you dared to swim in the pools beneath with confidence. The ocean opened up an entire new world even for a non-swimmer like me when I wore my goggles. I love the warm water!

This summer we *chose* not to live in the house across from the sugar factory! Actually, I'm not sure the house was still standing! Maybe the termites had finished it off! We had arranged to stay on a small college campus on the side of the Haleakala Volcano. The college was closed for the summer holidays. Again I was in charge of the kitchen, but this was old stuff by now. Once again the team was assigned to different churches and work.

The Congregational Churches would not allow us to work with them this time. With sadness, I was unable to go back to the children and people I had learned to love. We were not even allowed to visit the churches. So this summer I was assigned to work with the Salvation Army in Lahaina. The people in that church were Portuguese, so once again I had a new culture to learn. God was teaching me to see *people* and to love them. Although their culture might be different, they all had feelings, habits, needs, and desires exactly as I did.

That summer we did a lot of camping programs. We would take the children and/or youth to campgrounds along the coast and spend a whole week with them. Here we lived and worked together and really saw kids saved and taught in the way of the Lord.

We did learn enough about demons and the power of Satan that I will never again question the significance of their influence and power. There are many "menahoonies" in Hawaii. Those are the little invisible men that control rocks, eat pork and generally keep people in fear. They live in Haleakala Crater and on many big rocks going out to sea. If fishermen do not stop and pray in the little menahoonie building before going out fishing, they never come back. If you want to pass certain rocks along the highway and have pork in the car, you have to throw the pork out of the car, or you will not be able to pass. You are not allowed to take any pork into the crater or you will not come out alive.

On one occasion, we decided to take a youth group into the crater. It was a one-day hike to the first cabin where we camped and could explore the cares in the area. The second day we would hike out of the crater. The young people had warned us not to take any pork because of the menahoonie rock. With a wink, we assured them we would never do anything like that!

Since I was in charge of the food, I knew pork was the cheapest meat in Hawaii, so it was my choice to take. We could use the bacon with eggs, keep the grease to cook other things, and have pork chops with a wonderful pineapple sauce. A delightful menu! We hiked to the cabin with no problems. After exploring the caves for an hour, I decided I had better go back and start supper for the hungry crew. The cabins were completely furnished: dishes, matches, firewood, and all you needed for a *very* cold night in the crater. (Estimations of -20o late at night.) I got out all the food and dishes, put the wood in the stove, and looked for the matches. There were none. We had been assured there would be plenty! I about tore the place apart looking to no avail. Dutch then came in to help look. Finally the youth and rest of the team came.

It was then that the young Hawaiians realized we had brought pork. They began to cry and scream! "You will never find the matches! You have disobeyed the menehoonies, and we will all die!"

It was 7:30 and dark by that time. At 9:30 we still had not found the matches, and the fellows had failed to get a spark from rocks, etc. The youth were snuggled together with the few blankets in the cabin. It was beginning to really get cold. 10:00 and still no fire. The youth were weeping and could not be consoled. Finally we had a serious prayer meeting! As a team we felt the power of Satan. At 10:30, with tears, declaring that, "Greater is He who is in you than he who is in the world," Dutch found the matches wrapped in a towel, inside a large jar, in the farthest corner of the storage closet. With rejoicing we finally realized that our battle had been a spiritual one. Satan had been defeated, and two of those young people accepted Christ as Savior.

The menehoonie stories were real. Satan has power to convince people of the reality of menehoonies so he can keep them in bondage. Only with much prayer and the power of the Holy Spirit was Satan's work foiled. God is greater, but I learned that I fear battle with the prince and power of the air. I will never *seek* to do battle with him, but praise God, if it is ever necessary; He is greater than our foe.

It was near the end of that summer of 1958 that I, overworked and ill, ended up in the bed the story in the introduction. I was rushed to the hospital and found to have a fever of 106 degrees. With every method the doctors and nurses knew, they fought to bring my temperature down. I do not know what happened because I was unconscious; however, I was told that when the fever did begin to break, my sheets were changed five times in two hours, as they were soaked with my perspiration.

Test showed that I had a blood deficiency and was unable to fight simple diseases and therefore almost died of the flu. I was not well enough to fly home with the team as had been planned but had to spend two more days in the hospital. Two of the team members stayed behind, and together we boarded a later plane and flew to Los Angeles. There I was put on a plane bound for Denver, Colorado, to see a doctor. The team had gathered together the money to pay to fly me home.

So once again my family and I were brought together to be reconciled even more. My father was also sick. He had diabetes and was suffering from kidney infection. I was fearful that he would not live much longer, so once again I tried to share Christ with him. He was sick enough that he listened but was not willing to give his life to Christ. He began to share with me that he really didn't want to live anyway. I told him I loved him so much, I didn't want him to die! We cried together, but Dad still didn't feel that he was bad enough to need Jesus.

****

In weakness, knowing that I could now do nothing apart from Christ, I went back to school for my junior year. I began the year with no money, a sick father who still refused to help (and now really couldn't,) and a weak body of my own. The doctor had advised that I shouldn't return to school, but I felt I had to. So with my vitamins, medicine, molasses, a need of ten hours of sleep daily, and Christ, I returned.

I don't recall any outstanding events in my junior year. I know that I continued to work full time, and I put much more time into my studies because I now had courses in my major of education, which I loved. I had outstanding professors. One was the elementary education supervisor, Dr. Snapper. This man did not just love the subjects to be taught to children; he loved children. In fact, he loved people. He was a great man of God. He wanted his students to be able to use the work of every assignment he gave in our own teaching. There was absolutely no busy work. I learned so very much and could hardly wait to begin applying my new knowledge and skills.

I did work in a local church and tried much of my new knowledge on the youth and children I was assigned to teach. In Youth For Christ parties, I was also able to use my newly learned teaching methods to teach and strengthen the faith of the youth who attended.

    My Bible courses were outstanding. I had the privilege of sitting under the teaching of Dr. David Hubbard. However, that name was a bit unfamiliar to his students. He insisted that we call him "Dave" both in class and in public. He played volleyball on the beach with us, shared our sorrows, and was a real friend. His knowledge of the Word was strengthening to our faith and he taught in such a way that we all desired to be able to communicate as he did. Perhaps by example, he taught me as much about teaching as I learned in the courses on teaching methods!

    I continued to be active in choir and grew to love and know music better. My confidence was growing; I was no longer threatened by the wealthy and popular students, I had many, many friends, great men of God accepted me, I was growing in Christ.

    I had chosen a life verse; "I want to know Christ and the power of His resurrection and the fellowship of sharing in His sufferings, becoming like Him in His death." Philippians 3:10. The verse had become more meaningful in my life. I was learning what it meant to know Christ. The power of His resurrection was becoming clearer to me as I saw Him provide for me. I had experienced forgiveness and newness of life. I knew some of the fellowship of His sufferings; I had felt the criticism of fellow students, been rejected by some, suffered hurt in witnessing the poverty of many Hawaiians and migrant workers in California, and I had almost tasted death myself. I knew my life was just beginning, and I would learn much more about the things mentioned in the verse. But I took hold of it once more, ready for all God had ahead for me and confident of His grace and salvation. My weaknesses were becoming less worrisome, and I felt ready to go back to my family in Colorado for the summer, face what was there, and then return for my senior year and the insecurity of not knowing the future. God would continue to walk with me.

CHAPTER 9 – MORE TESTS

"Consider it pure joy, my brothers, whenever you face trials of many kinds, because you know that the testing of your faith develops perseverance. Perseverance must finish its work so that you may be mature and complete, not lacking anything."
- James 1:2-4

Uncle Paul wanted me to work at camp again. I was delighted. This was my ninth year at Id-Ra-Ha-Je. However in the middle of the summer, an opportunity came that Uncle Paul said I should take. A Rev. Drake had visited the camp and seen me at work. He was directing a camp in Arizona, and their youth director had just notified them that he would not be able to be at the camp. So, this Rev. Drake was frantically looking for someone to take that position. I was excited about the possibilities of serving in a new camp. Little did I know what was ahead.

When I arrived home from school, I was met by a desperate testimony. My father had grown very weak.

"I tried to commit suicide last night."

"But Dad, why?!

"I am a burden to your mom, and no one really loves me anyway."

"That is not true! You are very sick, but I'm sure you will be well soon. You cannot give up. Besides, I love you very much!"

"I know. That is why I didn't do it. I was in the bathroom with my razor, and then I realized you were coming home. So, I went back to bed."

"Dad, don't you also know that God loves you? Won't you accept Him? I really don't know how you could live without Him. He wants to help you."

"Oh, I did that."

"Did what?"

"Oh, you know. When I was a kid I went forward in the church."

"What do you mean you went forward? What did you do when you went forward?

"Oh, you know."

"No, Dad, I don't. Do you mean you prayed for forgiveness of sin and desired to follow Jesus?"

"Oh, not that. Just went forward. I really am not bad, you know."

With much more silent prayer, I did all I could to reveal to Dad the meaning of salvation, the need of forgiveness because he really did have sin, and the great desire of my heart that he would accept the Lord. It all ended with total rejection and a pathetic cry, "Oh, I don't need all that. I just need you, and now you are home."

With that Dad went to sleep.

But Dad was not getting better and had been hospitalized twice. I really didn't think I should go to Arizona. But Mom wanted me to go. What a thrill it was to hear Mom say: "I am beginning to understand why you girls (meaning me and my two sisters) want to work at camp and read the Bible. I think I am beginning to understand that God loves us and wants us to tell others."

When I pressed her, she shared that she didn't know when, but little by little she had accepted what she learned. She felt that she had been forgiven and wanted to follow Jesus as we were. I was so thrilled that I cried and hugged her. That turned the conversation quickly! We never showed affection in the family, and my hug unnerved her. She pushed me away and said "You go on to Arizona! If Dad dies, I don't want you to come back. I will be fine with the girls here, and when you come back we can talk about it. Now, I really mean that! I want you to go, minister, do what God wants you to do, and you must promise not to leave your work there just for a silly funeral." I knew Mom. I had to promise and brush aside the hurt caused by her seeming rejection of my joy in her salvation and show of affection.

At the end of June, I left for hot Arizona. I had expected a program somewhat like Id-Ra-Ha-Je. Wow, was I in for a surprise! Upon arrival I was told that there would be about seventy-five Indian youth and fifty white high school kids. I was it! There were no other counselors or helpers. I was totally in charge. I was to plan the activities, Bible lessons and everything else needed for the day. We would all join in the big meeting at night with the adults. I had just that evening to prepare to face all those young people the next day.

Well, we began the week and I was having a great time with the Indian kids. I was enjoying learning about their culture and observing their shy ways. It was fun trying to get to know them and their seemingly strange names. But they responded, and soon not only their *names* were precious, but *they* were precious.

The white kids were a totally different story. When we had Bible study, they would sit in the back, pass notes, and generally ignore the lesson. When we had fun times, skits, and games, they would refuse to participate. But the Indian kids were enjoying themselves and having a great time. I tried to talk to some of the white kids while they were on kitchen cleanup only to be ignored and finally told by one kid to just leave them alone!

Needless to say, I spent many late nights on my knees. I couldn't understand the rejection or indifference. I tried to pour all my love into the Indian kids and continued to try to include the whites. Finally God answered prayer.

It was Saturday night after the first full week of camp. I walked into the dish shed where the dishes were being washed. I smiled and greeted the four white kids that were there and asked if I could help. With that the gang leader, a girl, broke down crying. "No" she said. I said I really didn't mind, especially if she was not feeling well. I slipped my arm around her waist and asked what was wrong. Out poured the story.

"Oh, Ivy! We are so sorry! You really are neat, but we have been so mean! We wanted the other youth director to be here and when we heard he couldn't come, we asked my dad to direct. He said he just couldn't but that we would like you. We then made a pact that we would be as mean to you as we could so that you would decide to leave and Dad would *have* to be the director! We really like you, and we don't want you to leave now! Mr. Jones told us he was going back to Denver because an emergency had come up, and we just knew it was to take you back. Please don't go! We will do all we can to help you now, and we really like you. You have taught us so much, and you are so much fun!"

I had no intention of leaving, so I assured them that I was staying and welcomed the repentant kids. Wow, the next week was so great I can't begin to explain it.

I had been provided a bus to take the kids on a couple trips. We went to a beautiful river where we could swim and slide down the rocks over small waterfalls. We also planned a trip to the Grand Canyon where we would spend the day.

All the kids were cooperating, decisions for Christ were made, and we laughed together so much that our sides ached. We hiked into the Grand Canyon—to the halfway mark—thinking we could be back by 6:00 P.M. if we ran down. OH my! Don't ever do that! On the way out, about a mile from the top, I became so exhausted and sore I could not walk another step. Praise God that there were Indian kids along with us. Two strong Navaho fellows carried me out!

Another interesting thing happened. A fellow, who was a senior in college, appeared on the scene. Lane had been a camper there in years past and wanted to see how things were going before going back to Arizona State University. He wasn't very tall, only about two inches taller than I am, but good looking? You bet! He had a marvelous blond crew cut. His muscles were bigger than any I had ever seen. He loved to sing, and it seemed we were singing duets immediately. The kids thought he was great because they already knew him, and very soon they were all matchmaking. But the biggest shock of all was that he liked me! The rest of the week was exciting and almost caused me to forget why I was there!

The week ended; camp was over. Tears were shed as I parted with the youth group. Some of those young people became lifelong friends; one even enrolled at Westmont a year later because of our acquaintance. Lane decided to go to Colorado with me and see if Uncle Paul could use him as a counselor.

It was at Id-Ra-Ha-Je that I got to know more about Lane. He was a wonderful Christian, but I began to see pride and flaws in his personality that I just couldn't live with. He was *always* at least forty-five minutes late to everything. He spent a lot of time making himself beautiful; lifting weights, combing his hair, shaving, and showering. But he was *never* on time. I was *his* girl, not *a* girl! With his possessiveness, pride, and other character flaws, I knew he could never be a permanent part of my life. It took the whole next year—sending back the engagement ring, which had arrived by mail, and numerous rejections of his phone calls—to convince him that we really were not meant for each other.

Dad really was sick. He was back in the hospital, and on July 18th he died. He was only sixty years old, but he had no desire to live so he left us. I was glad I was there for the funeral. I was able to help Mom. My sisters were still a bit young—going into their sophomore and senior years of high school. Mom wanted Daddy cremated. But the funeral was still very expensive for us as Mom had been the sole support of the family for the last year. The impact of Dad being gone really did not hit me until the following Christmas when I came home and he was not there. There will always be that sad knowledge that he never accepted or felt the need of the Savior.

I gained a lot of maturity during that summer. Maturity really is the result of the trials we face, the testing of our faith and perseverance. Ahead of me was my final year at Westmont. Certainly it would be easier. Wrong.

****

I was to do my student teaching the first semester. Almost immediately I realized the school I was assigned to was much too far away to walk to. I knew there were no buses going to that area. I had gotten a sixth-grade class, which I really had wanted. But how to get there? Onto my knees I went. A sophomore friend from Colorado had a car. About a week into the year, he returned to Colorado. He didn't have the money or the stamina to work his way through the year when he really didn't like school that well anyway. He said he would sell me his car. Now understand, it was a car, but not in the best shape. He would sell it to me for the total of $1 providing I promised to pay in monthly payments of ten cents a month. That way he reasoned, he would receive the news of the school and at least get an occasional letter. I could not believe it but was thrilled with the proposition. I soon learned, when I drove into a filling station, to say, "Please fill up on oil and check the gas."

I also found out that somehow God had rigged the car to start only when it was pushed or rolled down a hill, and that it would run only when it went to school. Because my cash was very low, I obeyed and used the car only for student teaching and not for other activities.

Second semester was a bit confusing. The business office of school said that I had to work full time or would not be able to finish my last semester. They had to be assured of incoming money. They were trying to change their policies and have students pay in advance; however, because they knew of my struggles, all I had to do was produce evidence of a job and assurance of payment for that job.

On the other hand, the Education department said that I could *not* work the last semester of school because my class load was too heavy, and I would need to give full attention to the class work. To continue my education, I had to promise that I would not be working, or they would have to drop me from the major.

By now I knew that God had a plan. What it was, I was not sure, but again I was on my knees. About that time my mother sent me $400. That was the first and only money she ever sent. She truly did want to help me, and now that Dad was gone she was free to do so. She really wanted to send more, but that was all she had. Only heaven knows what a big blessing the $400 was to me. Mom was supporting me and God was supplying!

I heard Mr. Armour of Armour Star Meats needed a housekeeper. I applied and got the job. They provided a room for me. I worked on Saturdays cleaning their house and shining silver, and occasionally I babysat the three children when they went out in the evening! My new job slashed my Westmont bill to a minimum by cutting out the cost of room and board. I had proof of a job with payment. I convinced the Education Department I would be able to get all my coursework done since I had a private room, and this was not really a job but just a dwelling place off campus. They agreed! Praise God, I was almost "home." Indeed, in June of 1960, I was among the graduates of Westmont College.

CHAPTER 10 - GOD SOLVES MY BIGGEST PROBLEM

*"That is why, for Christ's sake,
I delight . . . in insults" (problems).
-2 Corinthians 12:10*

Devastation of all devastations! My education in a Christian University was finished, and I had not found the husband I had gone to seek! To be very honest, I had not committed that part of my life to the Lord. I'm not sure I realized that I hadn't, but it was true. I'm sure I scared away every available man by chasing him. And as you know from previous chapters, I was a bit picky. In fact, as with most of us, the guys I liked ran *from* me, and the guys I couldn't stand ran *to* me!

I had gone back to Id-Ra-Ha-Je again for the summer and found a young man I really liked. He spent a lot of time talking to me, and we played trumpet duets together. But he was usually asking me about Connie, my friend for the summer. I realized the problem. He wanted to be my friend to find out all he could about Connie. Again I was devastated! But I kept looking. I felt that I had to find a man at camp or in a Christian service place. I certainly would not be satisfied with someone that did not actively want to be in Christian service. Well, the summer passed and no one showed up.

I had been hired to teach a 4th-grade class in Simi Valley, California. I'll admit that this was the first place I lived that the scenery wasn't beautiful. Oh, you can learn to like a dessert place if you set your mind to it. But, as usual, it really was the people that drew me.

The first day of teacher orientation, I had asked the moderator to announce that I was looking for a place to live. There were over two hundred teachers in the room. Afterward an older lady, Ella, approached me and said that she had just rented a small two-bedroom house and would appreciate a roommate to help pay the rent. On further discussion, I found that she was a Christian lady who attended the Nazarene Church. She was also new to the district, having just come from the Pasadena area.

We taught at the same school, Santa Susanna, and lived within walking distance of the school. However, she had a car so we often drove together. After a few months of teaching, and saving most of my check (that seemed like a fortune), I bought a car. I felt I had really splurged; it was a white Comet with bright red seats.

My little Comet took me to the Baptist Church near the school and to many Dodger baseball games in L.A. Usually I had three of my students, Max, Richard, and John, with me. Because I felt the fellows were taking advantage of me, I had them pay for the gas, my ticket as well as theirs, and their respect for me grew.

It was a good year, I think! The school was experiencing real growing pains and was badly overcrowded. Each teacher had around forty-five students! I guess I didn't really realize that was an unrealistic number of students for a fourth grade class. I did remember that when I was student teaching I only had about thirty students, but I pressed on.

The sixth-grade materials I'd used in teaching were not suitable for fourth graders; consequently, I had an entire new curriculum to plan and organize. Being an artist at heart, I desired every one of my bulletin boards to be perfect. The principal insisted that the boards be changed every month, and he actually checked to see that they were. Papers to be graded piled high. Then, because my bulletin boards were always presentable, I was asked to do the main board in the outside hall. Needless to say, I was overworked and slowly going under. I would arrive at work at 8:00 A.M., and get home around 10:00-11:00 P. M. daily. I had sense enough to take a break on Saturdays and go to an occasional baseball game or do something with the youth from the church.

I took a group of the youth to Youth for Christ in Ventura, about sixty miles away. My roommate was *old,* I think near sixty. So I wanted to be with the youth all I could in my spare time. I was still looking for that husband, and I was lonely. All too soon I discovered the church I was in to be super legalistic; my lifestyle wasn't perfect enough for the leader and spiritual ladies there. One young man, a senior in high school (just two years my junior) was full of life and had recently become a Christian. He couldn't see why everyone was so uptight about having fun. Soon we were best friends. But because of loneliness, our relationship became serious, and the superintendent of schools found out I was spending a lot of time with this young man. I was told to sever relations with him or lose my job.

It was time to move on to a new church. Since I now had a car, I drove the length of the valley—probably 10 miles—to a little Alliance Church. There I met a precious couple and their two kids. Jim and Betty Leppard are special friends to this day. They took me in as a daughter, and my life settled down.

****

Pressure at school was mounting. Sometime into the second semester, the kids got the best of me. There were too many hours in the workday, too many new things to learn and prepare, and too many students to teach. Dad had always controlled me by yelling; in desperation, I tried it on the kids. It worked a few times, but soon they didn't like their teacher anymore and that further devastated me. Finally, one day when pressure had mounted, and my gimmick of yelling was no longer effective, I broke down and cried. Without my knowing, one student slipped out of the class and reported it to my principal.

A substitute was called in and to my surprise, I was asked to go home and rest for the remainder of the day. I was to come in at my leisure the next morning for an appointment with the principal. When I reported, I found that he had made an appointment in L.A. for me with a special friend of his who was a doctor. Perhaps I needed to be checked out physically. I had broken down in class.

I am not fond of doctors! But what could I do? The appointment was made, and my principal had asked me to go. When I arrived, the doctor checked me over, then we sat down to have a friendly chat. At the beginning he asked me some very embarrassing questions, in fact, insulting ones! He wanted to know about everything that hurt. Well, I had been having some pain in my private parts, and so he inquired about my sex life. He was very surprised to find that I had never had sex with anyone. (It turned out that hemorrhoids caused my pain!)

After what seemed like an eternity, he told me there was absolutely nothing wrong with me except I was overworked. He would report to my principal and send me the bill. Yes, the bill. It was $50. I had never paid out so much in my entire life! You must remember this was 1961, and doctor bills were usually about $10 a visit. I had been sent to a psychiatrist! This was indeed an insult. When I shared my feeling with my principal who was my good friend, he apologized. The school was trying its best to make the classes smaller. He begged me to forgive him for thinking I may be psychologically unsound and to please come back and teach next year.

****

Summer rolled around again. I wanted to go home and see my mother. We were beginning to be much closer since she now understood my love for the Savior. She also was beginning to understand more about the Lord. She had changed churches and was getting some good teaching. I would work at Id-Ra-Ha-Je again as it really was my home.

Many exciting things, both good and bad, were going to happen at camp. Had I known what they were, I'm not sure I would have had the strength to stay and face them. But often what we think is the worst in life turns out to be the best the Lord has planned for us.

Howard was a friend at camp that I greatly admired. His sister was one of my best friends. I had been in her wedding. He had bright red hair, much redder than mine, played trumpet, and was a counselor at camp. We often played our trumpets together, and thus were often together. I was still man hunting and thought he was a pretty good choice. I had only been at camp a month when Uncle Paul asked me to do another job.

A team of students was coming from Biola College to work for the summer. The week they arrived, the camp was packed (about five hundred kids in three different programs.) The team had to go to a small camp in Frisco, Colorado, for their orientation. Since I had been at camp for ten years, Uncle Paul felt I was well equipped to train them in the culture of the mountain town and the campers. He wanted me to go with them to Frisco. I would only be gone from camp for a week.

I was not very excited. I was getting to know Howard. I had been asked to be the recreational director for main camp with about 350 kids and was teaching a large class. I was in my element and wanted to stay. I was not in the least bit excited about orienting a group of college students. But, with pressure, I went.

The team from Biola was made up of three guys and eight girls. Jim was short, and immediately thought I was great—again someone I wasn't much interested in. Dick was much too quiet, not very good looking, and not interesting at all. Dave was a winner. However, he was engaged to a girl back at Biola. No problem! In fact, that would even be better. I was after Howard, and Dave was safe, so we could really have fun together—in the few spare minutes we had.

It was a good week. I grew to really like these students and realized I really wasn't much older than them since I always had been a year younger than my classmates. Pauline became a special friend, and the three of us, Pauline, Dave, and I had great times during breaks.

The following week most of these students were sent out in teams with Uncle Paul's teachers to the mountain town of Colorado. Two were to go to camp and I got to go back too. I stepped into my role as teacher and sports director. Dave and Dick had been assigned to camp. Right away kids were drawn to Dave since he was a macho guy and fun. But as the week went on, I noticed that the kids were slowly growing tired of Dave and his rah-rah. Groups of kids were gathering around Dick and having serious talks and then breaking out in laughter. Finally, my curiosity got the best of me, so I decided to find out what was so attractive about this counselor.

The kids told me Dick really helped them with their problems. He understood them better than anyone at camp. He was helping them to come to know the Lord better and finding solutions to their problems. And, they said, best of all, Dick was funny. Even during serious talks, he would crack a dry joke, and the kids were impressed. He really had a droll sense of humor.

Upon returning to camp I noticed something drastic had changed with Howard. He was cold toward me and always was too busy or otherwise occupied when we were supposed to play duets. I was hurt but didn't really know what was going on. I was having so much fun with the campers and was so involved with my teaching and sports that I really didn't have time to think about it.

The next week Dick and Danny Coffee, a young high school student, were sent to Alma, Colorado to teach there. About mid-week Uncle Paul asked me to check on them to see if they needed more books or any help. I was a bit excited about it because I wanted to know more about Dick—that kind of not-very-good-looking guy—that the kids seemed to like so much.

So off I went. I must have been more excited than I realized. About halfway there, a policeman pulled me over!

"Madam, are you going to a fire?"

"Oh, (gulp) no sir. Was I driving too fast?"

"Well, you were going about sixty in a forty mile an hour zone."

"Officer, I'm so sorry! I really didn't realize . . . "

He began to chuckle. He was friendly enough and just gave me a warning. Since this was my first time to be stopped by a policeman, I was quite embarrassed.

Dick and Danny were doing fine. They had enough books, had about eight students in the Bible school, and had enough food. In fact, they were elated. They were told that every child in town was coming to their Bible school. Many of the towns in Colorado are small.

When I got back to camp, Uncle Paul called me into his office. He was very serious. I'm not sure he had ever reprimanded me before, but he was so sober and concerned that I didn't know what to think. Some counselors had come to him and shared great concerns for my conduct. To be very honest, I do not remember all of the accusations, but I do know they were not true or were vastly exaggerated. Uncle Paul laid them all out before me.

I could see immediately that most of the things were just not true, and I could prove it. Uncle Paul allowed me to call in some of the people concerned and found that, indeed, I was not guilty. I had made some minor infractions in the rules, and he asked me to go and make those things right. Uncle Paul didn't want to tell me who had made the accusations, but when I pressed him he told me it was Howard. To this day I do not know why he told such lies—so turned against me. The only explanation I ever got was from his sister. She suspected that he was very jealous of me and was trying to exalt himself by putting me down.

    I admit I'm a forward, sometimes almost pushy person. My sisters thought me proud and unkind when I didn't get what I wanted. There was further hurt when I went home for the weekend. My mother reprimanded me. She had received word from my sisters that I was being obnoxious at camp, and they wished she would refuse to allow me to return to camp.

    Well, I did return. Uncle Paul had asked that I would. But I was a hurt, meek person, and found it difficult to work. I was also very angry with Howard. I didn't know quite what to do. Insult! It drove me to my knees. Probably the place I should have been all the time. Finally, due to hurt and confusion, I gave that part of my life—men—over to the Lord. In fact, I was so adamant about it that in the following evening service when it came time for testimonies, I stood and said that I was happy to announce that I was engaged. The shock in the audience was apparent. "Yes, I am engaged to Jesus Christ and will give my life fully to Him."

****

    The following September 1961, I went back to Santa Susanna to teach fourth grade once again. This year was next to heaven. Indeed the principal had worked on the problems. I taught from 7:30 A.M. to 1:00 P.M. and had only twenty students! There was another teacher in my room from 1:00 P.M. to 5:00 P.M. teaching a second fourth-grade class. Not only was the day shorter, the children fewer, but also I had a fellow teacher to share the work of the bulletin boards.

    At home and relaxed on the first Saturday back in Simi Valley, I looked out the window to see a flashy Mercury pull up in front of my house. Who in the world was this? It must be a friend coming to visit my roommate, Ella. I waited to see. To my surprise, out of the car stepped Dick, that somewhat plain fellow from Biola who had been at Camp Id-Ra-Ha-Je. He had gotten my address before returning to California. The truth of the matter was that he hated Convocation—the opening assembly of school, which is what was happening at Biola that day. Just before he left his home in Santa Cruz, California, to return to school, a garbage truck had backed over his Volkswagen and damaged it badly. His dad had allowed him to drive the family car to school and would deliver Dick's Volkswagen as soon as it was repaired. So, possessing a big, beautiful car, he had decided to take a drive. He didn't know exactly where to go, but then realized Simi was just sixty miles away from Biola—the exact distance he wanted to drive. On the way he had stopped to see another friend, a girl, washed the car, and then drove on over the hills into the valley. I was very surprised, but pleased.

We had an interesting day. I showed him the valley; we visited the areas popularly used in western movies; we had a pleasant time. Well, a fellow can't come see a girl just once, so he asked if I would mind if he came the next Saturday for a date. I accepted and wondered what would be ahead.

That was the beginning of dates every Saturday, with the exception of the one he got his wisdom teeth pulled, was swollen up like a chipmunk, and decided to miss until he looked normal again! He was a very considerate fellow. With time I found out he was from a solid Christian home, was a natural leader, did have a very dry wit, and was loved by many. In fact, Pauline warned me not to fall for that guy! He could get a date with any girl he wanted, and therefore he was fickle! I think she was slightly jealous.

After about two months, I knew this guy was for real, and I couldn't find one thing about him I didn't like. He loved the Lord more than anyone I knew. He asked Ella, my roommate if he could spend the night so he could help out on Sunday at the Alliance Church. He didn't stay every weekend, but often. My friends, the Leppards, loved him from the start. Here was a man their kids looked up to and respected.

Remember, I mentioned that I am a bit bold—sometimes even obnoxious? Well, one evening in the moonlight, Dick and I walked down the railroad tracks next to our house. If you know me at all, you know I love beauty—especially the moon! I was beginning to fall—not off the track—but for him. Yes, I was standing on the tracks and was just at his level. Well, I kissed him. There isn't any excuse--I just did it! To this day, he will not let me forget it. Our first kiss, and I initiated it!

Dick asked me to come to his home for Thanksgiving. He wanted me to meet his family—his dad and mom, a sister, Linda, and two brothers, Paul and Joe. I had visited Mt. Hermon in my Westmont days and was delighted to be able to go back to Santa Cruz. I also wanted to meet his family, especially his folks. I had been told that most often young men would turn out like their fathers, and I wanted to see what his father was like.

He picked me up immediately after school; we had four hundred miles to drive in his little convertible Volkswagen. About 7:00 P.M. I fell asleep. I had been keeping my typical long hours at school. About 9:00 P.M., I woke up and asked where we were. He said we were near King City, which is about eighty miles from Santa Cruz. But before we could say any more, we both screamed as the sight of a large cow strolling slowly across the road frightened us. Dick knew if he swerved it would mean sure disaster; so with the brake on and both of us bracing ourselves, we hit the cow head on!! It came up on top of the car, through the convertible top, and onto our heads. When the car came to a stop, the cow rolled off on the passenger side and moaned. I felt so sorry for the cow, I couldn't think straight. Dick helped me out of the car, and I continued to be concerned for the cow. "Just like a woman! My poor car is totaled, and she is thinking of the cow!"

But God had saved our lives with that of the cow, which was later shot to be put out of its misery. On impact, the cow jammed both front fenders so tightly against the wheels that, had the cow not been on top to hold us down, the car would have rolled and we probably would have been killed. From the farmhouse of the nearby ranch, we called Dad Otto. He, Paul a freshman in high school, and Joe, an eighth-grader, came to meet Dick's new "friend."

Needless to say, it was a very dramatic meeting. In the next few days, I became acquainted with a man of God who was so much fun, so kind and loving that I began to hope that sons did turn out to be like their fathers, and to *greatly* desire to become a part of that family!

I went home to Colorado for Christmas. I thought that when I returned, Dick would either propose or break off our relationship. It was getting so serious I knew something had to happen one way or the other. But for the first time in my life, I had not been chasing. I had honestly given this part of my life over to the Lord.

Uncharacteristically I kept quiet and didn't even tell my mom I had a boyfriend. I wasn't interested in chasing anyone at camp. At the winter retreat, I had a great time.

When I returned to California, I received a telephone call.

"Hello, Ivy?"

"Why, Hello, Dick!"

"You, got back okay?"

"Yes."

"Well, I will see you tomorrow about 5:00. Bye."

I had never received such a short phone call! I just knew that it meant that our relationship was over! I must have cried for two hours. But finally I came to realize that God must have a better plan, and once again I trusted in His wisdom although I didn't understand it at the time.

Dick came the next day, Friday. His sister dropped him off; I was to take him on to L.A. after our weekend together. Things seemed to be the same as before I went to Colorado. He greeted me with a big hug—after his sister left—and he was excited about seeing me. We spent the weekend together, with Ella acting as our chaperone, ministering at the church as usual. Then, on Sunday evening, I took Dick back to Biola. As we were saying goodbye, I began crying. I was just so confused I couldn't hold it any longer. I always have been one to confront and solve problems as soon as possible.

"Ivy, what's wrong?"

"Dick, why was the phone call so short?"

"Oh, that! I'd just made two other long distance calls on my folks phone and had talked too long. When I started to call you, my dad said, "You make that short!" I knew that if I said anything other than that I was coming, I'd start talking and not be able to stop because I'd missed you so, so much!"

Then the tears really came—tears of joy. When I told him what I had thought and how sad I had been, he was so sorry. Then he said: "Ivy, I didn't want to do this tonight, but I think I better say something. I *am* going to ask you to marry me! But I wanted to wait until I had the ring, and that won't be for a while yet because I just don't have the money!"

With the exception of my salvation, I think that was the happiest moment of my entire life! Here was a man that loved God more than any other I had ever met, he loved me, and I absolutely could find no fault in him—not one thing that I would want to change. I was in heaven, and all the way home that night I continued to tell the Lord how wonderful He was! God loved me and was concerned about the biggest things in my life as well!

****

The next year and a half was the longest year of my life! Dick was only a junior in college and he wanted to wait until he was closer to graduation and would be at least twenty-one. In the months that followed, his mother also assured me it would be best to wait. I was not so sure I felt that was true, but I tried to be patient.

At Easter time I found myself in Santa Cruz again. The only fight we had in our entire courtship happened the weekend before Easter. We had been looking at engagement rings. When I hinted that I really would like to have it before summer so I could show everyone I really was engaged, Dick turned into someone I had not met before.

"Ivy, I can't get the ring before summer! I'm going to be working to save for it. I'm really sorry but that is just the way it is!"

I was crushed! He had never spoken to me in that tone of voice before, and I didn't like it. I spent the rest of the day apologizing and trying to assure him that it was OK, but he didn't seem to be comforted. He was very angry; I tried my best the change the atmosphere. Finally, he settled a bit but I wondered what would happen in the future when we disagreed!

Well, the week at Dick's folk's home was wonderful. This was the most beautiful Christian family I had ever met. The boys were funny teenagers, and Linda was a sweet, laid-back gal. She was a freshman at Biola. They were member of Twin Lakes Baptist Church, a very large church in Santa Cruz. The pastor there, Rev. Roy Kraft, was one of the best speakers I had ever heard. It was a wonderful week and I couldn't have been happier. I think it was a Friday night after going out for supper—we came back to the house and in the backyard, in the moonlight, Dick asked me to marry him and put a ring on my finger! For the first time, and probably the last, I was speechless! I only cried.

Dick had tried to rig a tape recorder to record my reaction, but it hadn't worked.

"Boy, it sure was okay that I didn't get the recorder to work! There was only silence after I asked you to marry me!"

Which was true.

"Hey, Turkey, why all the flack and sternness about the ring?" I asked.

"That was tough. I had to put on an act to convince you I couldn't get the ring this soon. I wanted to surprise you. You made it terribly hard for me to keep up the act that I was angry about you pressing me! I just hope I don't have to do that kind of act again!"

I can count on one hand the times in our thirty-three years together that I have seen Dick angry. I had not needed to fear what he would do when we disagreed in the future.

****

That summer I went back to Colorado and Id-Ra-Ha-Je. I had the ring on my finger and was the most relaxed person there. I probably did the most effective counseling of my entire career. I spent a lot of time writing letters. In August Dick came for a visit, and we had the privilege of standing up for my Mother and her new husband. Yes, the night I called Mom from Santa Cruz to tell her I was engaged, she said, "Well, I have a surprise for you too. I am engaged, but I will be getting married sooner than you! I'm getting married in August."

That summer Mom and I prepared for her very simple wedding. My two sisters, Dick and I were the only ones present besides the bridegroom and the preacher. In Mom's home, Mom and Mike became husband and wife.

I had another year at Santa Susanna. Although Dick and I were together every weekend, I felt it was still too long until my wedding. I planned the best I could for "that blessed day" which was a whole year away. I knew that I would have only a month to prepare when I returned to

Colorado and during that time, Mom would make my dress. I set to work making all the bridesmaid dresses.

When I arrived in Colorado the 7th of June, I had lots to do. Because I didn't have much money, I arranged all my flowers and made the bouquets. I also created and baked my own wedding cake. It was the first wedding cake I had made. My aunt taught me how to make the frosting flowers and gave me a few pointers in putting a wedding cake together, but she refused to do it. "Too big a wedding." She said.

It was big—about three hundred people. And it was the most beautiful wedding in the world. Of course!

We honeymooned in Yellowstone Park. Dick's folks had made reservations at Old Faithful Inn for us. It was superb, but I'd recommend if you really want to see a place, don't go there on your honeymoon!

After the honeymoon, we went back to Santa Cruz. Dad Otto was a contractor in Santa Cruz. Dick worked for him during the rest of the summer. Dad was putting up three apartment buildings on the lot next to their house. We lived in the finished one, and they worked on the other two.

I won't go into details about the time I baked three chocolate cakes before I got one we could eat, or the other similar incidents that happen to all new brides—I was no exception. The church in Santa Cruz held a beautiful reception for us; I got to wear my wedding dress again since most of the people there had not been able to come to the wedding in Colorado. Many wonderful lifetime friends who continue to support and pray for us to this day came from that church.

In the fall it was back to Biola for Dick. He had one more semester to complete. I got a job in Garden Grove, California, and drove to work every day from Buena Park. We lived five blocks from Knott's Berry Farm, about five miles from Disneyland, two miles from Biola—right in the heart of southern California. Since I had to complete my year's teaching contract, Dick entered Talbot Seminary in January; but as the year progressed, he decided five years of Biola/Talbot philosophy was enough. He would transfer to Denver Seminary the next fall.

CHAPTER 11 – SURVIVING SEMINARY

*"That is why, for Christ's sake ,
I delight . . . in hardships."
-2 Corinthians 12:10*

We didn't think they were hardships! Perhaps because we were so happily married and full of love, we didn't even realize we were poor. Of course, we were poor only by American standards; now we realize that compared to the world we really were well off.

Dick was sure he needed to go to Colorado for his seminary training. I wasn't too happy about it since I would take a $2,000 a year cut in pay. I was earning $6,000 a year in California, but instead of getting another raise in California, I would drop to $4,000 a year, which was the starting teacher's salary in Colorado. On the other hand, I was happy that we would be close to my family and perhaps be able to work at Id-Ra-Ha-Je in the summers. So, we packed our things and headed for Colorado.

The company where we rented a trailer made a very big mistake. Because they wanted our business, they said our little Comet was adequate to pull the trailer we rented. Every earthly possession we had was in that trailer. On the top right-hand corner, we carefully stowed our box of Lennox China. We left at 5:00 P.M. from Buena Park, California, intending to drive all night. We did not want to go through the heat of the desert in the daytime. Joe, Dick's younger brother, was along to spend the summer at camp. We tried, about midnight, to sleep by the side of the road.

"Ivy, do you think there are snakes out here," asked Joe.

"Oh, I don't think they will bother us, Joe," I said.

"I have heard that they love to snuggle close to a warm body," he remarked.

There was a long pause. Now I too was hearing every noise around. For some reason, I couldn't get my eyes to close.

"And, Ivy, I think most of the snakes in the desert are rattlesnakes."

We both woke Dick and carried on!

Early the next morning we were about a hundred miles from Las Vegas, Nevada. Have you been there? There seems to be about one hundred miles of straight road going slightly downhill toward the city. It didn't take long on this long downhill stretch for the trailer to begin to try to pass the car. Dick stepped on the gas to try to right the problem, but that just caused the trailer to go faster and become even more determined to pass the car! At seventy miles per hour, Dick realized he could never outrun the trailer and slowed. The trailer was tenacious. Finally, Dick saw it was, indeed, not only going to pass but cause us to crash! He put the brakes on as gently as possible to try to slow the car. By God's grace, when the trailer did jackknife, flip, and grind us to a halt, we were pushed up against a small bank. Just fifty yards down the road, the embankment because a gully. Just a few more yards would have meant disaster! There sat our car, smashed up against the bank with the trailer upside down right beside it. We were okay, but what about our things? Yes, that upper right-hand corner was the corner that was smashed!

Dick hitched a ride into Las Vegas, and about five hours later he returned with a rental truck—rather big and old! A wrecker came along to help right the trailer.

"Lord, the things in this trailer are yours. You know we have no money to get new ones. We just trust you to care for them and take care of us."

When the wrecker turned the trailer over, we could hear hundreds of things shatter; our hearts sank. After a loud crash, the trailer was once again sitting right side up. Slowly we began to unload it and put things into the truck. We were totally amazed! Each item seemed to be intact—only a few scratches and some small dents. Scattered through everything were pieces of glass. Then we remembered. The last thing Dick had put into the trailer was our full- length mirror. That was what had broken and sounded so terrible as the trailer was righted. We examined the box of Lennox China and found only one cup broken! To me it was a total miracle—a confirmation that the Lord was indeed watching over us and would supply not only our needs, but take full care of us. This was our first bout with material things. Did we really believe people are to love and things are to use? Many in our society live as if things are to love and people are to use. I know God used this accident to gently admonish us to hold things lightly.

Joe and I went ahead in the car, and Dick drove the truck. We did change once, and I had my opportunity to drive the big rental truck. It was short lived. I do not enjoy driving those large trucks. Finally, the last hundred miles into Golden, Colorado, where we were to stay with Mom and Mike, Dick took over the truck and Joe and I headed into town in the car. We arrived about 5:00 A.M. and thought Dick would be in shortly. He didn't come until the next morning about 8:00 A.M.

As he was lumbering up the western slope of Loveland Pass, very near the top where the hairpin curves are tightest, the truck stalled. He could not get it to start and finally ran the battery down. He put the truck in reverse gear, rolled it precariously backward down the road, and lifted his foot from the clutch. Now close your eyes and picture his predicament! Hairpin curves, one of the highest passes in Colorado, steep cliffs on the downside, narrow roads. He did succeed in starting the truck, but I asked him to spare me any more details of the incident! Then, as he was coming down the other side, the truck ran out of gas! The gas gauge said the tank still was half full. The gauge lied! There was no gas. So, trying to make his way through the hills, he refrained from braking on the downhill, hoping to coast up the next rise. About 3:00 in the morning, and I think as an answer to prayer, he made it into the town of Empire. All the gas stations were closed tight. He tried to sleep in the truck, but it gets extremely cold in those mountains at night. Of course, I had the suitcases with the extra clothes in the car. The night was long and quite unbearable! He finally got home and found a very worried but happy wife.

****

We spent the summer at Id-Ra-Ha-Je directing the Teepee Camp. Heap Big Chief Dick and Squaw Ivy had a great time. We actually lived in teepees and taught the kids to cook their own food on open campfires. We had meetings in the longhouse and played capture the flag. The summer was a real adventure, no hardship at all.

Then school began. My job was at a school in Denver just two miles from the seminary apartments. In those days many educators thought children did better in school when grouped with others of similar I.Q. levels. They called it homogeneous grouping. I was given a fourth grade, a precious group of kids all with very low I.Q.'s. I was to bring them up to grade level. The boy with the highest I.Q. was the son of one of the teachers there. His I.Q. was 75. An average I.Q. is around 100. I had 32 African-Americans, one Hispanic and one white student, but their I.Q.'s and ethnicity were definitely not the cause of the hardship that I faced.

I loved those kids, and it was a delight to see them begin to enjoy school and actually learn to read and advance. I was no miracle worker—I just love kids. They were indeed learning. But the principal of that school had a very jealous streak! She began to demand things of me that no teacher could do. Maybe she was so insecure that she didn't know how to handle me, or maybe she was prejudiced. I was one of three white teachers. The other two white teachers were quiet and non- threatening to her Afro-American background. Anyway, even some of the Afro-American teachers noticed what was happening and came to my defense. That just made matters worse. As the year progressed, she even would come into my class and berate me in front of the students.

I had grown very close to the teacher who was the mother of the best student in my class. She loved the Lord dearly and encouraged me a great deal. I shared with her that I was expecting my first baby. She was so pleased and excited for me that she couldn't keep it from her son. News travels. Somehow it got to the principal. She rushed into my class and started screaming.

"So, you thought you could go against policy and continue teaching when you were pregnant! I knew you were dishonest from the first day!" she shouted.

I knew that at twenty weeks pregnant I would have to quit teaching. I was only eight weeks pregnant and had already told the superintendent that I would have to quit in twelve weeks but wanted to stay on as long as I could. Praise God, I was able just to hold my tongue and let her vent her wrath. I'm not sure how I managed it, but when she was finished, I calmly said, "The superintendent knows."

We spent the summer at Id-Ra-Ha-Je directing the Teepee camp again. The only real struggle I had there was the refusal of staff and campers to allow me to play baseball!

"I can't pitch to you because your stomach is so big, I can't see the plate! And besides, I'm afraid I will hit you!" So I took up archery.

What an experience when Tim finally was born! We had come back from camp on Saturday. Sunday Dick wanted to go to the Billy Graham crusade in Denver. I didn't feel like sitting in the hot sun, so I stayed home. The next day Dick went to the seminar for crusade counselors because he had really enjoyed his time at the stadium. I went to my weekly appointment with the doctor. The doctor was very anxious about my condition. I had gained forty-five pounds, much to his dismay.

"But Doctor! I am starving myself! It can't be fat! (And by the way, after Tim was born I ate everything in sight and lost fifty pounds!)

"You may be right. You are full of water. I'm concerned. I really think we should get on with it and induce labor."

He told me I was to report to the hospital in one hour. I called Dick out of his seminar and he met me at home. We called my mom before going to the hospital.

I was given a drug at 1:00 A.M. About three hours later when nothing seemed to be happening, the nurse came in.

"I want to give you a pill to help you relax. It may cause the labor to go faster," she said.

I knew very little about medicine, hospitals, or any of that since this was my first pregnancy. Didn't I *have* to obey the nurse? I took the pill, and the next time I woke up, it was 10:00 in the evening. I was in a different room and didn't remember anything. I felt for the baby, but my stomach felt strange. It was still very big but flatter.

"Had I had the baby or what? Oh, dear!" I thought.

When they knew I was awake, Dick and Mom came and stood beside me. Mom said, "So, how do you like your big baby boy?"

A baby boy! I couldn't have been happier! They told me I had almost died during the birth because of the tearing. I was given blood to replace what I had lost. I was so naïve I thought all new mothers received transfusions!

I was now twenty-six and had many friends my age who already had three kids! In 1965, twenty-six seemed to be a bit old to start on a family. But even then we knew we would face a tough time financially. Not only did Denver school district have the policy that forbade teaching after twenty weeks into pregnancy, but also, new mothers could not return to teaching until the child was one year old. So, our second year at Denver would be tight. I would not be working and Dick would have to work part-time while doing his studies as well.

    But that was one of our most glorious years. Since I was not working, I had time to entertain, and we got to know many of the other couples at the seminary. The fellowship was precious, and the loving but struggling testimonies of the other students helped us grow. God certainly did supply and bless. At Christmas, we received a large box of food from the school. We knew it was a policy to give boxes of food to those in need; but as I stated at the beginning of this chapter, we didn't even know we were one of the "struggling students in need of food." We felt very loved.

    We spent the following two summers at Teepee Camp again. This second year we moved out of the teepee's to a small cabin. With a nine-month-old baby boy, the teepees were a bit hazardous.

****

    Those years at Denver were priceless. We fellowshipped with Dr. Vernon Grounds and learned of his true humble nature, his love for the students, and how he spent his time. He got to know every student, took them out for breakfast, listened to them, and counseled them when he saw a need or they desired direction. We sat under Dr. Raymond Buker, a veteran missionary and statesman. Dr. Gordon Lewis taught theology in such a practical way that it has never left us. Although I didn't take his class, I typed all of Dick's reports, so I learned much of what he was taught. The required homework was a study of each theological subject—God, Jesus, man, sin, Satan, etc. He asked the students to list at least ten verses to support each section. These verses came from every part of the Bible establishing the truth of the subject. Mrs. Lewis, who spent time with the wives, kept us laughing, loving, and thoroughly enjoying our days there. All of the professors poured values into our lives that have stayed with us and molded our ministries.

****

Entering our third year of Seminary, we needed money. So what else was new? However, God had always provided and would continue to do so. Dick was invited to be the youth pastor at Fruitdale Baptist Church and we would live in the apartment above the church's gym. That would take care of our housing. They paid a small salary, and I could substitute teach. My mother lived just five miles from Fruitdale and was willing to babysit Tim on the days I was called to work. I got my love for kids from my mother, and she was delighted to be able to take care of her redheaded grandson. I knew he would be in excellent hands; thus went the year.

Our stay at Fruitdale was a blessed time and one of growth. We worked under Rev. Mark Bubeck, a devoted man of God. He taught us many things. We learned the value of expository preaching—preaching through an entire book rather than topics. We saw in him the hours of prayer that are needed in ministry. One of the most valuable lessons I learned is that we do not need to be defensive, for God protects us from false accusations.

There was another young man on staff who was a bit wild. He went behind Dick's back starting rumors and causing problems. Some of the parents believed him, and I was livid! I began defending my husband and telling people what a big liar this young man was. Soon Mark called me into his study.

"Ivy, you do not need to defend your husband. Let God do it."

These were some of the wisest words I received, and I have never forgotten them. I had seen God defend the work Dr. Grounds was doing and protect his ministry. Now I would see God at work in Dick's life.

I worked with Baptist Youth on Sunday evenings. We had children from first to sixth grades in the group. We had a great time pretending we were in the army— the army of the Lord. We gained our medals by memory work and had routine marches and singing. It was great fun.

It was this year that Dick and I became interested in missions. We didn't think we would go into it fulltime because we had always dreamed of being camp directors someplace in America. However, we reasoned, it would be good to have a short term in missions so we would be better able to direct youth into Christian work of a cross-cultural nature. If you're a camp counselor, you need to be able to counsel young people about all the areas of service to which God may call them. We believed the great commission and wanted youth to carry the gospel to the entire world. However, when it came to us working cross-culturally, we knew we couldn't because neither of us were linguists.

While applying for missions work ourselves, the idea hit me that we could pretend in Baptist Youth that these kids were also becoming missionaries. So I set up a program for the children that involved memory work and awards. We pretended that we were in school. To complete junior high school, they learned certain verses. In high school they wrote reports about Christian living beside memorizing verses. We continued with college—again assigning activities to them. Finally, they pretended to apply to a mission agency, write the government for passports, and procure visas for the country they had chosen to minister in. We had language learning courses and even presented a program with the children telling about the work they would be doing. The kids loved the program and learned a great deal about missions. Since then my book on *Missions Alive* has been published and used many times in many places to acquaint kids with missions.

But after the Conservative Baptist Foreign Mission Society received our application, we were asked why we were applying for short-term work. We had all the qualifications for full-time missions and full-time people were really needed. After much prayer, we decided that we would go to Uganda, East Africa, fulltime. After all, the language there was English, and if it didn't work, we could resign.

In February Nancy was born. She was another little redhead. The birthing was super, as they say in England! It was different in the doctor's examining room this time . . . "That was a contraction! Why didn't you go to the hospital instead? You should have met me there instead of my office!" scolded the doctor.

"How should I know, Doctor? It didn't seem bad. I just thought I had a cramp!"

Well, again I called Dick to meet me, this time at the hospital. In two and a half hours Nancy was born. I threatened to sue the hospital if they gave me any drugs! I wanted this child by natural childbirth and with no help. And that's how it went. I was happy and excited about being able to see some of the birth. Nancy was a bit red and misshapen, but she was my girl! She was small and not as difficult to deliver as Tim had been. I felt so good I could have walked back to my room. Had she waited nine hours and fifteen minutes, she would have been a leap year baby. I'm kind of glad she didn't.

Pastor Mark and his delightful family had been called to minister in another church, and Dick had become interim pastor. After a year of service, we said good-bye to the church and moved to California. Our training at the seminary was complete. We were faced with the joy and responsibility of finding churches and people to support our work in Uganda—both financially and in prayer. We used to call that "deputation;" these days it is called "home assignment." We would raise most of our support in California where Dick's folks lived and we already had a base of friends and church acquaintances. However many people from Fruitdale remained some of our best supporters through the coming years.

****

We met a young girl at camp who had been abused by her father. Her mother also ignored her, so Barni came to live with us the last year we were in Colorado. She attended Rockmont College and was a big help at home.

She babysat two-year-old Tim and our newborn, Nancy, and did many household chores while we continued our work at the church. Barni was like a daughter to us, and we loved her a great deal.

When we moved to California, Barni came with us. The happy part of this story is that while she was in Santa Cruz, she met a handsome young man, and in August, before we left in November for Uganda, she was married. I got to make my second wedding cake! Our funny, little redheaded children were both in the wedding. It proved okay, but Nancy struggled getting down the aisle. She was only eighteen months old! Their parents were rather proud of them and thought they looked rather cute; so did their Grandma!

The year we spent in California in deputation raising money to go to the field, was a fantastic year as we got to be with Dick's parents. We had had three years with my family and now had one with his.

We were told to bring all the shoes the children would need for the next four years! I now know how very foolish that was. We should have realized kids in Uganda buy shoes there because it is required all students have shoes and uniforms to go to school. Indeed! It shows how foolish we sometimes are. Before we left, we took a picture of the twenty pairs of shoes lined up on the floor. Boy, did we miscalculate! Nancy wore hers out fast, but Tim not only grew slowly, he never wore his shoes out! He used only three pairs of shoes in the four years; the others were lost in our eviction! But that comes later.

PART III

GO!

CHAPTER 12 – FINALLY TO UGANDA

We had all of our support in November 1969 and so headed for Kampala, Uganda.

Winston Churchill said, "Going to Uganda was like the story of Jack and the beanstalk . . . instead of a beanstalk, you climbed up a railroad and at the top was the pearl of Africa." Great Britain had colonized East Africa: Kenya on the Indian Ocean became a colony while Uganda—just west of Kenya—became a protectorate. Uganda is located on the equator but is four thousand feet in elevation. Having Lake Victoria—the second largest lake in the world—as one boundary, contributes to a moderate climate of between seventy and eighty degrees year around. It reminded me a great deal of Hawaii: tropical climate, birds, flowers, and temperature.

Africa is divided into two large groups of people—the Nilotic (those which originated in the Nile Valley) and the Bantu. These two groups of people are as different in customs and languages as are Western (U.S. and European) and Eastern (Chinese and Japanese) customs and languages. Thousands of individual tribes exist within the Nilotic and Bantu groups. The Nile River flows north out of Lake Victoria forming natural boundaries in Uganda in between the southwest and the north. There are twenty-six different tribes in
Uganda. Each tribe speaks its own language. The tribes in the north are generally nomadic and are very different than the people of the southwest.

The northerners are Nilotic in origin and tend to be hunters and fighters. The Bantu people in the southwest are farmers and live much more peaceably. Kampala, the capital of Uganda is near Lake Victoria in the south of the country. This was to be our new home, working among the Baganda tribe.

We would eventually learn that Bantu tribal languages are similar in some ways. In all of them Mu=one person; Ba=many people or the tribe; Lu=the language; Bu=the area where they live; and Ki=their culture. So a Muganda (single person) of the Baganda (plural of the singular Muganda and also the name of the tribe) would speak Luganda (the language of the Baganda tribe) in the Buganda area of Uganda, and his or her music and traditions are Kiganda. The language of other tribes follow the same pattern: The Lusoga language is spoken by a Musoga of the Basoga tribe in the Busoga area, with Kisoga customs; and Lunyankoli is spoken by a Munyankoli of the Banyankoli tribe in the Bunyankoli area with Kinyankoli customs. Wow! Now I know why language learning is so difficult!

"You know, Dick, it won't be hard getting adjusted to Uganda since everyone speaks English," I said.

That was the beginning of one of many, many shocks! Yes, in Kampala Ugandans spoke English with an African accent. I was able to understand the Ugandan English very soon. But on Sunday when I tried to talk to the whites from the U.K., I found I could only understand about 50% of what they said.

"Hello, I'm Ivy Otto. What is your name?"

"Vari glod ta meet yo. Ma naam is Gram."

"Excuse me?"

Our dialogue is just too hard to write, but after about six tries the poor fellow said, "Hove yo Hard of Billy Gram? Wall, tha's ma naam! Gram!"

My biggest shock in Uganda was to find people were *real*. Now I know you must think that is crazy, but somehow I had been given the impression that these people were like small children in big bodies. I thought they knew nothing and somehow were below me. Wow, what a shock! These people were intelligent and much better mannered, kinder, and more loving than almost anyone I knew in America. In time I learned a million things from them compared to the ten I taught them. I learned compassion, care, politeness, and real interest in people. It didn't take long until I knew God had brought us to the right place, and I hoped we could stay here the rest of our lives.

Our huge yard was more fun than a big park because we could do in it what we liked. Tim, who was four now, could build things, look for insects and butterflies, play Robin Hood in the trees, and invite the neighbor kids over for even more fun. Nancy was always close behind although she was only two. We had a big shepherd dog, and when she gave birth to eleven puppies, things really became exciting.

We decided we would try to learn Luganda, the most commonly spoken language in Kampala. We sent Tim off to a school in hopes that he would learn Luganda since he would be with pre-school kids all day. He did learn a lot of math but not language—the kids just wanted to touch his flaming red hair and laugh a lot. He didn't do much talking! I remember him coming in one day with tears in his eyes after playing with his friends.

"Mommy," he said, "we have been here four months now, and I am still white! When will I turn black?"

He was struggling with the language and culture as much as we were. We found we just weren't learning Luganda. It was suggested that we go to Nairobi, Kenya, where we could take a course in Swahili. Perhaps if we learned Swahili, which is comparatively easy, we would also acquire a language learning method we could apply to our study of Luganda. None of the team members had managed to learn Luganda except one who had grown up in Zaire. We agreed to go.

We could only get into the course for one month but decided that was better than nothing at all. Better than nothing at all? What a time we had! Learning even an *easy* language is not easy. Anyway, it was not easy for us. Things just didn't stick in my head. I would repeat and repeat, but they still sounded like nonsense syllables! Dick was doing better than I was. He was enjoying the teachers and seemed to have a better ear for the language. I tried to write everything down. I was depending on the paper, my eyes, and reading, not on listening. Strange how American culture depends so much more on writing than on hearing. Maybe that is why we have such a hard time listening to one another!

While we were struggling with the language, we were having fun with the other students, who, like us, were struggling! Our kids were having a ball! They got to meet other missionary children and play, play, play! At the end of the day they had so much to share. Nancy played with Steve. They were both only two years old. It was hard to get those two to stop playing and come to eat.

Our language study center was in a British guesthouse, run by a proper British lady. I often wonder how she ever survived the many uncouth Americans she had to deal with. Children were fed at 5:00 P.M. They had to eat with a proper large spoon. I once snuck a teaspoon from teatime into my pocket so two-year-old Nancy could eat a bit easier. But disaster of all disasters, she saw the spoon and immediately whisked it away!

The children were not allowed at the adult 8:00 P.M. supper. Now you tell me what you do with a two-year-old and a four-year-old while you eat your *proper* supper! We could never get them to sleep before we had to go eat. Night after night they stood at the door, parting the curtains so they could peep in. And of course *she* caught them every time, and we got a scolding! Well, after one month of study, the children had survived, the hostess had survived, but we had only learned enough Swahili to say Hello, and give our names. Actually we knew we had to have much more study. We went back to Kampala and then on to Bukavu, Zaire, to study there with our mission's missionaries.

****

Ruth Kreutter was our teacher and did a great job. She taught more like the teachers in our American schools. Dick was totally exasperated in the classroom as he doesn't do well with reading and writing, but I thrived. I didn't learn how to speak or understand what I heard, but I could read and write up a storm. Dick was not doing well in class, but he loves people, so he talked to the workers and neighbors and soon was communicating with all of them.

I will stop here to say that after one month in Zaire, and one more back in Kenya, plus three more months in 1988, my husband is fluent in Swahili. I get by!

****

While we went to language school, Tim attended a Luganda speaking kindergarten; he had two months in a British/English kindergarten in Nairobi (separated by one month in the American kindergarten in Zaire) and finished up the year in the Asian/English kindergarten next door to our home in Kampala. I'm not sure if all this confused him or if it was a good experience. I do know that he got top grades through all of his schooling that followed, seemed to really love school, and certainly has a bi-cultural heart.

Was it possible that dropping one-third in salary, over-turning a trailer, having little money, struggling with a jealous principal, almost dying in childbirth, being humiliated by a co-worker in a church, and finding that I knew very little when comparing myself with another culture and language could all be hardships? Perhaps. But as Dick's dad had always taught us, "You choose your attitude," and we chose to look at these things as lessons that would teach us about the tremendous grace of God. Also, when we look at Jesus, the circumstances dim. Furthermore, when we look back, we see that it was these very things that made us strong—that taught us to persevere. You know " . . . suffering produces perseverance; perseverance, character; and character, hope. And hope does not disappoint us . . . " Romans 5:3-5.

    Dick spent our first three years in a program called TEE, Theological Education by Extension. He had four training centers and traveled to those areas to train pastors. They would learn and discuss a subject. The following Sunday in their churches, they would preach what they had learned. Dick then returned the following week to hear of their struggles and how things went. Problems were solved and the next lesson taught.

    I spent most of my time with children and youth. Since they were the future of Uganda, I felt strongly that we needed to mold the children. As we then walk with youth through decision-making, these children and youth can grow to be good leaders.

    Looking back we certainly were rewarded in this endeavor. The leaders of the church in Uganda today are the youth and children that Dick and I disciple and worked within 1969-1973.

CHAPTER 13 – CHAOS IN UGANDA

"That is why, for Christ's sake, I delight . . . in persecutions . . ."
-2 Corinthians 19:10

  One evening, leaving Tim and Nancy with a babysitter, Dick and I left to visit a Ugandan couple across town. We were in our new blue Fiat and enjoying the car very much. We drove into the yard of our friends, and a car pulled in behind us. As we started to get out of our car, two men jumped out and grabbed Dick. He quickly turned on the cutout switch and got out. They ordered me out of the car. One of the men, holding his gun, jumped into the driver's seat and tried to start the car. Meanwhile, as I stood back and watched, the man holding Dick ripped the watch off Dick's arm. The man inside the car yelled, "This thing won't start! They have cut off the power somehow." The man holding Dick let go, lifted a panga (a machete type knife with a blade about two and a half feet long by six inches wide) and brought it down on Dick's back, but he had turned the blade so it hit Dick broadside instead of on the sharp edge. He raised the knife again, looked up to be sure it was facing with the blade down, and struck again. God graciously had moved Dick to the side, so when the blade came crashing down through space it hit the ground. By now the man inside the car had jumped out. He ordered Dick to get back in and start the car. Dick did this and then threw the cut out switch again. By now the men were not only afraid their robbery job was not going to work but were also angry. As Dick climbed out of the car, one of them pushed him back in and ordered him the start the car again. When the car was running, they threw Dick out onto the ground, jumped in, and drove away. Just then another car pulled out of the trees; the second man jumped into it, and it also drove away.

  As we saw our car drive away, we were indeed shaken. We turned and went up to the door of our friends and knocked. Our friends were afraid to open the door because they had seen the thieves coming and had locked things up tight. When they finally realized we were alone, they let us in. We cried and prayed together, reviewing the details and praising God that He had indeed protected us. We then had our friends take us to the home of fellow missionaries and rehearsed the evening once again.

This was just a beginning. Of the six couples on the field, five of us had our cars taken at gunpoint. We were afraid to drive anywhere. We felt thieves must be following us at all times, seeking to take our cars. Thus began a three-month period in my life where I was continually filled with fear. I was afraid to drive anywhere. Our car was found, but it had been totaled. The insurance company paid our claim and we purchased a new white Peugeot station wagon. But any time I drove it, my hands would grip the steering wheel until the fingernails bit into my skin. I was constantly watching in the rear mirror, and if it looked like anyone was following me, I would make weird turns to test them. It took me a long time to get to my destinations!

But even at home, I was becoming afraid of everyone. When people would come, I was almost afraid to open the door. I was eating regularly—in fact a lot—but I was losing weight. I had a favorite tape that I often played. It was "I Looked for Love" by the Ralph Carmichael Choir. It amazes me that even today when I hear that song I get that funny "fear feeling" in my stomach. But with it I am reminded of how great God is and how He helped me work through it. But let me continue with the story so you can see how God did work.

Fear continued to dwell in me. One day in desperation, I cried out to God to deliver me! "Please, give me a verse or something that will alleviate the fear." He gave me 2 Corinthians 10:5, "We demolish arguments and every pretension that sets itself up against the knowledge of God, and we take captive every thought to make it obedient to Christ."

Now, how did that help? The Holy Spirit showed me that my thoughts were only of things that *could* happen, not reality. No one was really taking my car. When thieves *had* stolen our car, I had felt the presence of God and there was no fear; in fact, I felt direction and a sense that He was with us. We had both been amazed at the peace we had experienced during the ordeal. But now that nothing was actually happening, I was fearful. I was living in the "what if" stage and God does not give us strength, protection, and peace in an unreal situation. He only gives these things when we need them. Was my God big enough to be with me "if and when?" Yes, He had already proven that. Then I also realized from the verse that I was to take captive of these thoughts by being obedient to the promises of the Savior—He would be with me, I was to trust Him. From that day the fear began to disappear and whenever it would come, I would shout, "Get behind me, Satan. Jesus is here and *if* thieves come to take our car, our belongings, or to kill us, I will have the strength to bear it!" It worked!

****

We did not know that January 24th was a religious holiday. The Hindu Temple was very close to our house. The Indian people loved to have celebrations, and they usually used many fireworks. About midnight the fireworks began. After hearing them for over three hours, we began to wonder how we had missed knowing about such a big celebration. The fireworks continued during the rest of the night, and finally, about 6:00 A.M., subsided.

Thankfully the children slept through it, so Dick awakened Tim to get him ready for school—now attending first grade at Nakasero School, a British school in Kampala. As he left, we noticed how quiet the streets were. Most of the time, there were hundreds of people walking to school, work, and the market. But there was no one. So Dick went on, and I returned to the house with Nancy. When my house girl came in, I could see the fear written on her face. What had happened? Debra did not know English, but in simple Luganda, with lots of signs, she made me realize that the fireworks had not been at the Hindu Temple, but was gunfire about five miles away!

I ran immediately to the radio to see what I could learn. Music. More music. In fact, for two hours . . . music. Not even *one* commercial or announcement. Wisely, I finally turned on the shortwave radio and looked for the British Broadcasting Company. I learned that there had been a coup in Uganda. President Milton Obote had gone to Singapore for an International Conference and while out of the country, Commander Idi Amin had taken over the country by a military coup.

Dick had not returned. In fact, by 7:00 P.M. that evening, neither Dick nor Tim had returned. I was becoming *very* anxious. But I began to pray and trust that God was in control. Finally at about 10:00 P.M., both Dick and Tim returned. The soldiers had stopped Dick and they graciously allowed him to go to the home of the Holmes and wait out the day. Tim was still with him and so had a delightful time playing with the five other children on the property of the Holmes and Paulson's.

Dick and I turned on the radio and heard that Idi Amin was now the President of Uganda, and the country had been freed of Milton Obote. With that, the city went wild!

Milton Obote had systematically been sending soldiers into the homes of people of the Baganda tribe, (the tribe we worked with in Kampala) killing the members of families sitting around their tables. People knew of friends and relatives disappearing. Children reported having seen their parents brutally killed in front of them. It was no secret to the Baganda people but a well-kept secret from the world. No wonder the people went wild. Celebrations began and Amin rode through the town in his open jeep waving to the people and shouting that they were free! He released about fifty people that Obote had put in prison. He made arrangements for the Baganda king's body to be brought from England so it could be buried in Uganda. King Freddie had died in exile in 1970, and Obote had refused to allow the people to bring his body back to Uganda.

For about a year, the Baganda tribe celebrated and praised Amin for his takeover of the country, because he had freed them from Obote. But before long it became apparent that he had little regard for the Baganda. He was not a Muganda (a member of the Baganda tribe); in fact, he was from the small Kakwa tribe from the north—a warring and hunting tribe. He had only a second-grade education, but had been trained by the British as a military leader. When Amin started killing Bantu people just as had Obote, they realized Amin was not their friend.

We are not certain what the reasons were for the change in Amin—disease, pride, greed, revenge—but, indeed, he did change. Stories began to spread that he too was killing Baganda people in their homes. People in government began to disappear. Then doctors and teachers began to disappear. Because Amin was Muslim (only 6% of the country's people are Muslim), he began building a tower called a minaret, on the historic site of Laggard's Fort. From a minaret (a muezzin) a man calls the community to prayer. (Amin's tower still stands unfinished and unused. The builders miscalculated during construction, and from about two-thirds of the way up, the tower leans so much it is unsafe. Amin did not have enough money to correct the mistake and finish the tower. It is the dream of the Muslims today to correct it.)

Things also began to happen to us. There were five couples ministering to the Baganda. The mission's team decided Dick and I were to move south to a town called Mbarara. We would learn the language spoken there—Lunyankoli. But rather than begin our language study immediately, we were to take our furlough in America first. It was feared that if we took our language training and then went on furlough, we'd forget everything we learned before we could us it. So, we left for our six-months in America in June 1972.

There are many benefits to being a missionary. One is that when you travel home, you can often stop off at places that you wish to visit. It was at this time that we fulfilled a dream we had. We first visited friends in Ethiopia and then went on to Israel. It was a glorious experience. A professor from Denver Seminary and his wife were in Israel, and they agreed to show us around. We stayed in the Church Mission Society Guest House just inside the city walls of old Jerusalem. From there we traveled around the city, out to Jericho, Bethlehem, the Dead Sea, and finally to the Jordan River and the Sea of Galilee. It was a wonderful experience to walk where our Savior had walked.

We then went on to Greece to visit Corinth. Our children went swimming in the Mediterranean Sea. We had to stop in a small shop by the sea to buy a dress for Nancy and pants for Tim so they could travel on the bus in dry clothing. The beauty of the area, and the thrill of seeing the New Testament places were more precious than we had dared to imagine. We had planned to stop in Switzerland, a long time dream of mine because of the book of *Heidi*, but it became impossible due to airlines schedules.

****

During our six months in America, the Dobras, a missionary couple that had served with Conservative Baptist in India, were assigned to Uganda to work with the Indian people that lived there. They had been unable to get a visa back into India after their furlough. Frank and Alma were given three-month visitors' visas to Uganda—time to work on getting a work permit.

Dick and I had a great time in America, but we were anxious to get back to Uganda. It was now January 1973. So we began to pack up our things. Telegram! "Do not come now! Amin will not allow you back into the country. He has banned some groups from the country and your coming may alert him to the Baptists." Okay, so we waited. Two weeks passed. Could we come now? The answer came . . . Yes! Oh, joy, we are now on our way. Whoops! "No, do not come now. He has closed the border. No one is going in or out!" Again we waited.

I don't remember how often this happened, but it happened too many times! Finally, in April, we decided to go into Kenya, the country next door and wait there. Then, if and when the border opened, we could enter. As it was, it opened when we arrived, and so we continued our journey into Uganda. The next day it closed again!

Whew, back in Uganda. But it was tough! The Dobra's were leaving. They were going to move to Kenya because Amin had refused them a work permit and their three-month visa was running out. Then the Paulsons decided to go with them. Had not the pastor they were working with been threatened and escaped to Kenya? People were saying that because Hosea, the pastor, had disappeared, the army would come to Paulson's place demanding news of where he was. There was just too much pressure, so they followed the Dobras to Kenya.

Our other fellow missionaries were also facing problems. The Laurences had returned to America for their regular furlough, but they had not been granted a return visa to Uganda. The Holmes were requesting a renewal of their visas. Since they had been in Uganda for two terms, they were hopeful visas would be granted. The Hurlburts had joined Campus Crusade and were transferred to Kenya. In one month the Holmes visas and work permits were rejected, so they packed up their things to return to the states. That left only the Prigodichs and us.

Every day was a new adventure . . . threat. More groups were being banned. More people were disappearing. Then it was announced that the entire Asian community was to be sent away. Hundreds of these Indian and Pakistani people were third generation Ugandans. Where would they go? They were Ugandan citizens. They had no other home. Many of them packed their things and took them to the airport to be shipped to India or

England, only to have them looted! Many things disappeared. These 60,000 people were told to be out of the country by August, three months from the time of the announcement.

How did Amin decide all these things? Visions and dreams. Visions and dreams are a common source of direction for Ugandan people.

People were disappearing, being killed; threats were being published in the newspaper, and there was a growing fear. But we continued to trust our Lord. God would show us what to do.

At one point we bought airline tickets to Kenya for our two children. We gave instruction to our friends that if we were ever picked up or disappeared, they were to put the children on the East African Airways and contact the Paulsons in Kenya. That isn't what happened.

For months the pressure grew. Amin ordered that all muzungus (white people) were to stay wherever they lived. No one was to move. Therefore we could not move to Mbarara. Dick continued training the pastors in four different areas of Uganda—all about forty miles from Kampala. It was the TEE Program—Theological Education by Extension. I continued teaching youth in the hostels in Kampala. I also helped out at the English speaking church, Kampala Baptist.

Tim was now in the third grade at Lincoln School, an International School mainly for expatriates—the word used all over the third world to refer to people in a country that are not its citizens. I was teaching there to help with the tuition. Tim's teacher was a wonderful lady. She had been crippled by a serious brain tumor, but she loved the children and had fought to get her health back to be able to teach. Tim loved his class and was truly excited about school.

Nancy was in the first grade. I had wanted her to be in kindergarten, but the teachers had determined that she was too advanced for that class. They put her in the first grade where she was the center of attention. With only 12 in a class, it is easy to be the leader—especially if you have an outgoing personality and red hair!

Although on the outside it looked as if we were OK, inside the pressure was building. Everyday continued to bring more threats. Finally in October, for my birthday, we decided to take a camping trip to Lake Nabugabu. This was one of our favorite spots. We could swim in the lake, do a bit of fishing, and just relax in our tents. There was a forest close by, and one of Tim's favorite hobbies was to collect butterflies. The butterflies of Uganda are outstanding—especially in a forest.

The second day, as we walked down the path of the forest, a villager who did not speak English met us. Usually we greeted people in Luganda because we had at least learned how to say hello in that language. But this man did not respond in the friendly and excited manner usually shown by the Baganda when a muzungu spoke their language. In fact, he was hostile and began shouting and chasing us! Was Amin's attitudes rubbing off on the population? Now things were really getting bad!

****

The first Friday in November 1973, Ray and Nina Priodich decided to go to Kenya for a long overdue vacation. They packed their car and headed out. We bid them a safe journey and returned to our house with a bit of anxiety. The American Embassy had pulled out of Uganda. When the ambassador went to Amin to inform him that all American business would have to be sent through the West German Embassy, and that he himself was leaving, Amin was furious!

"All right! I will confiscate everything you own!"

But to his dismay, he found that the majority of the American community had left and that the Ambassador was the only government member still around. The Ambassador had sent his family and things back to America and had destroyed or sent all of the official files. There was nothing left for Amin to confiscate!

****

Dr. Webster, director of CBFMA, was coming to Nairobi, Kenya. Prigodichs were there on holiday, so they planned for our meetings to be held in Nairobi. We bought our tickets in Uganda with East African Airways. We were to leave on Thursday the following week to meet the team there in Nairobi.

Saturday I delivered the large wedding cake I had made for Lazarus and Lois Seruyangi's wedding. I was so proud of this huge cake. It survived the ride in the car to the church and fed the nine hundred people in attendance. It was a gorgeous wedding and these were very special friends. Today Lazarus is the President of Nairobi Evangelical School of Theology in Kenya and Lois is one of the teachers. She is a nurse and so helps in that capacity as well.

    Sunday we went to church as usual. Christopher, one of the leaders of the church, came to us that day and said, "Why, I thought you would be gone. You are the only missionaries left and even most of the Americans are gone."

    "Christopher, God has called us here. We will stay until He tells us to leave or carries us out!"

    Monday Dick had a meeting with Lazarus. Lois had to be back at the hospital, so the honeymoon had to be postponed. Tim, Nancy, and I went off to school for a typical day of learning and teaching. Dick had our car, and I was using the mission's Volkswagen. Tim wanted to go home with a friend, and I allowed it. Nancy and I started for home. When we drove into the yard there was a car there.

    "Hello, gentlemen. Can I help you?" I asked the two men who waited in their car.

    "Where is your husband?" one of them asked.

    "I don't know. He had meetings today and didn't tell me exactly where he would be."

    "Where is your car?"

    "My husband has it."

    "What is the license number on your car?"

    "I'm sorry, I don't know."

    "When will your husband be back?"

    "I don't know?"

    "Don't you know anything?!"

With that, I knew these two men were not visitors from any of the churches. So, I did what all good Ugandans do. I invited them in for tea.

"No! We will wait in the car!"

Oh, my! Now I knew for sure that this was not a good sign. *No one refuses tea!* Nancy and I went into the house. We told Teddy, our house-girl, what had taken place outside. She did not know what to think, but she began to cry.

"I just know that these men are here to take you to Luzira!"

Luzira was the prison to which many people were taken and then never seen again.

After an anxious wait of about one hour, a young man came running into the yard. He came to the house and announced that Uncle Dick was at the Scripture Union House with Lazarus, but that two men had arrested him. I was to come quickly!

I went outside to the men waiting in the car and told them that I knew where my husband was. I would lead them to him if they liked. I then walked out of the yard, down the street, passing about three houses, to the Scripture Union House. The men with the car followed me. Inside the house I found Dick. The two men with him went outside to talk with the men that had followed me.

"Honey, it looks like this is it. I have been arrested and I'm sure they will take me to jail, keep me for three days, and then take all of us to the airport." (This was the pattern the government had been following when they sent expatriates out of the country.) "They have already taken our car and asked where we want to go."

"Okay," I said, "I will go ahead with the plans we made. I will distribute all of our things we had promised to people, go to the bank and get our money, and pack up the things we want to take home. I'm sure glad that we made those lists and are ready."

It didn't happen that way! The four men took us back to our house. It was now 5:00 P.M., and they told us that at 6:30 they would take us to the airport! Just like that!

I almost panicked! I asked if I could please borrow the Volkswagen they had taken from us to go and get my son who was at a friend's house. We could not leave Uganda without our son! This they agreed to, and I rushed the fifteen minutes away to get Tim. I hurriedly told the mother that the Uganda Central Intelligence Agency had picked us up and they were making us leave the country *now!*" I asked her to please tell the school the next day that I would not be in to teach and let them know what had happened

Back home I had only one hour to pack. What would we take? Without money to pay for extra baggage, we would be able to take only forty-four pounds apiece. In all of the rush, I even forgot to look at the lists we'd made earlier. Teddy was crying hysterically! She just knew we were going to Luzira—that we were going to be killed. We had three high school girls living in the servant's quarters of the house. I tried to rush cake pans and decorating equipment to them, keep our children quiet while asking them to choose their favorite toys, rush information back to Scripture Union House, and pack—needless to say, thing were in chaos!

Cecilia was a young high school girl that lived in the servant quarters. This was her home while attending school in Kampala. If ever we could not find Nancy, our four-year-old, we knew she would be with Cecilia. Nancy loved her and her food!

Cecilia came in to help us in all the chaos. We knew that she would certainly try to get some of the things we had to the right people. The ladies I had trained to make wedding cakes would not be able to do so without the equipment. Cecilia knew these ladies and which people had been taught to play the accordion, the trumpet, and the two guitars we had. Actually, she had a very calming effect on all of us, and we bowed our heads to pray about the crisis we were facing. Soon we had done all we could do in one hour's time and were in the car with the two policemen.

What do you say to a policeman when he offers to buy some of the items he sees in your home as you rush around? Or to the policeman sitting on your bed while you pack? Or to the comments by the men, "We are really sorry about this. We see that you really do care about us, but we have our orders." Or "Why didn't you get Ugandan citizenship papers? I'm sure you could stay then."

How can a mother forget the tears in her son's eyes as he says, "Mommy, President Amin wouldn't be doing this to us if he knew how much we love his people, would he?"

At 7:30 P.M. these men walked us into the plane that we bound for Nairobi, Kenya. They stood beside us in the plane until it was time for take off.

****

Dick was angry. In fact, in all of our years of marriage, I had never seen my husband angry until now . . . and this was a *big anger!*

"God, you have been beaten this time!"

Dick lost about five hundred books—the entire library we had slowly built over the years in seminary. Commentaries, dictionaries—some worth over $50 apiece. All of his seminary notes were gone, the many Bible studies he had prepared for the men, his tools, his car, and everything that had become ours over the years.

Tim lost his toys. He saved only his butterfly collection, a few matchbox cars, and his Lego. Nancy had her doll collection, but what would happen to Simba, our big husky dog, and what about Nancy's little kitten? Who would care for them?

I lost all the china we had gotten at our wedding, the handmade blanket that Great Grandma had made for Nancy, our picture albums of the first eight years of our married lives, my musical instruments—although these had been passed on to friends. The silverware Dave Kraft had given us was gone (as was Dave who had died of cancer just five days before). Dick and he had been high school friends, leaders in their church and Youth for Christ Club together. Then they had gone on to Biola and both continued at Denver Seminary. Memories, memories. I think this is what brought the sorrow, the despair for me. But Dick lost his ministry: the men in whom he had invested so much love, knowledge, and time, and many years of work.

As we sat on that plane for the hour it took to get to Nairobi, we discussed what we were to do. Dick was so angry he refused to pray. We had our tickets to go to Nairobi on Thursday of that week. Since this was Monday evening, we were just four days early for the meetings.

When we arrived in Nairobi, we got off the plane rather than continuing to San Francisco where our tickets would have taken us. (These tickets were what the Ugandan government gave us in exchange for about

$40,000 worth of goods!) We got a three-week tourist visa for Kenya and registered at a hotel. From there we called our folks to tell them what had happened. The next morning we contacted the Prigodichs who were already in Kenya. We decided to wait the week out and see what steps to take in Kenya.

Win Hurlburt, our good friend now with Campus Crusade, suggested that we get Kenyan work permits and work in Nairobi. We went to the American Embassy to get new passports. With these Win went to the Kenyan government to try to get our permits. The Kenyan officials insisted that they needed to see our original passports. With further discussion and knowledge that we had been deported from Uganda, a Kenyan official advised Win to tell us to continue to the states. Were they to see our passports with our deportation stamps from Uganda, they would be forced to deport us from Kenya also. At the time Uganda, Kenya, and Tanzania were in the "East African Community" and worked together.

Next we tried to go to Zaire. But when we applied for a Zairian visa we found we had to apply from our home country, not from Kenya. We would have to return to America to get that visa. So our fate was sealed—we would return to America in two-and-a-half weeks time.

We were able to go to East African Airways and get refunds for our Thursday flights, so we at least had a little bit of money. Thursday Dr. Warren Webster arrived and we began our meetings. It was a sad time. Ray and Nina Prigodich telephoned their lawyer in Uganda to ask him to have all of their personal items sent to Kenya by train. They would be able to get a Kenyan work permit, and would relocate in Kenya. We would have to return to America, look at other fields or resign. I was broken-hearted. Dick was angry. But as usual, God had a wonderful plan.

CHAPTER 14 – R AND R IN AMERICA

"That is why, for Christ's sake, I delight . . . in difficulties . . . for when I am weak . . . "
-2 Corinthians 12:10

Back in America. What would we do? If we stayed with the mission we would have to relocate. (Called "redeployment" today!) Or we could resign. Then what? Well, first we had to find a place to live and replace all the things we had lost. Or did we?

"Ivy, how many times must I re-teach you lessons?"

This question was from the Lord. I had thought I'd lost everything before . . . on the road into Las Vegas. He had said then that people were to love and things to use . . . not things to love and people to use. Yes, I did remember.

"But Lord, that time the things had not disappeared. They really were all there, intact, so You didn't have to replace them"

"Am I so small I cannot replace a few things?"

"No, Lord. Forgive me and help my unbelief."

Thus began the miracles of recovery. Our churches soon heard of our dilemma. Money began to come in. The mission would allow us to raise $10,000 to replace a car, furniture, clothes, toys, you know, all that stuff that we each think we need.

But beyond that God provided in two other wonderful ways that have meant so much more to us. We moved in with Dick's parents in Santa Cruz, California, until we could find a place to stay. One day the doorbell rang. I went to answer it and found a deliveryman standing there with a guitar case and a trumpet case.

"There must be some mistake. No one here has ordered these things," I said.

"But Madam, a certain music shop here in Santa Cruz asked us to deliver these things to this address. There is no charge. They said they were giving these to some people that had lost these same instruments."

With tears of joy I took the two cases and thanked the man. When I called the music shop to check it out, it was true. We were the couple who had just been deported from Uganda, Africa and had lost everything. The owner felt that this was one way he could show how sorry he was and help us out. I was so happy, I shouted! Believe me, we thanked that man, his shop, and told everyone we met!

Even better is what happened when Jeane Kraft, the wife of our good friend Dave, came to see us. She brought a large suitcase. We visited awhile and shared the story of her loss of Dave and the years of struggle they had been through with is cancer then she asked us to tell our story. It was difficult to do because we realized that her loss was so much greater than ours. But after a time of sharing and then praying together (and a lot of crying as well), she gave me the suitcase. In it was Dave's accordion. I could not believe it! We had lost the set of silverware that she and Dave had given us at our wedding to gain his personal accordion. I could not have received a greater gift. Even today that accordion is here in Uganda, doing the Lord's work! Whoops, there I go again, getting ahead of myself and revealing too much of the story.

****

Joe, Dick's younger brother was off at school. He and Chris, Joe's wife, were in L.A. at the Physical Therapy School, and he offered us the use of his little house in Santa Cruz. It was a bit small for four of us, but we turned one room into two rooms by using a curtain. Tim moved in one side and Nancy the other. We were given or bought the bits of furniture we needed and were soon settled. But the real work was in deciding what we would do next.

The mission asked us to visit our churches to report what had happened and to raise the $10,000. We while we traveled on weekends, we inquired into a few of the fields our mission was involved in. Hong Kong seemed good but with further investigation, it looked like the team there was struggling. Part of the problem was that although English was used by the people there, it was not used enough for them to understand the gospel in English. We knew what that meant! Serious language study! We knew that the Chinese languages were by far the most difficult to learn! For two people who were "non-gifted linguists," we decided to look further.

Spain. Didn't the mission want to open a work there? Perhaps we could learn Spanish. Dick had had some Spanish at Biola and it was at least related to English. Maybe we could do that. We fired off a letter to the mission volunteering to be the couple to open Spain. They replied they really desired someone that already knew Spanish. If they found a couple that already knew Spanish, we were welcome to work with them. Well, the months passed, but that couple did not appear.

Believe me, all of this searching had been bathed in prayer. It seemed that God was saying the door to missions was closed for now, and we were to resign. With great sorrow, we accepted the fact. But we still didn't know what God wanted us to do. Hey, maybe it was camp work as we had originally thought. We had the mission experience and certainly could help counsel and guide youth. And yet, we had no peace and no direction as to what camp or where.

****

I had wanted a third child for about five years, but nothing had happened. Maybe it was the stress of language learning—cultural learning. I'm not sure, but I didn't get pregnant. When Dick tells the story, he says that we had made a deal not to have another baby. We had a boy and a girl. Since we were very busy with the work in Uganda, certainly we could do with just two children, the perfect family.

After we arrived back in the states, and after the excitement of Christmas, Dick brought up the subject.

"Honey, I know leaving Uganda has really been hard on all of us. I also know that we are no longer in Uganda and so you may think our deal is off. In other words, I know you have wanted a baby. Are you sure about this?"

"Absolutely!"

"Well, I have been thinking. Since we are in such a state of flux, and we certainly don't know what we are going to do, don't you think two children is just right? You know we have both a boy and a girl?"

"Oh, Dick, I thought you were going to tell me the deal was off!"

Then came my tears, and moans . . . all that go with a great disappointment. When Dick saw how truly devastated I was, he suggested that we try to conceive for two more months . . . *only!* Then he would have a vasectomy so that this subject and the stress of it would no longer be in our lives.

I prayed! Boy, did I pray!

And it happened. I got pregnant! I had been 3 months pregnant with Tim before I even suspected, and then the doctor had to tell me I was not sick but pregnant. It took a while before I realized what was happening when Nancy was conceived. But this one . . . I knew. I just knew! And sure enough, at my doctor's visit the end of January, I was told a baby was on the way! Dick really wasn't unhappy about it, just relieved that his thirty-five-year-old wife could have one last child and the controversy of our family size would be settled forevermore!

****

I guess it was about seven months later when one of our churches contacted us. They knew our dilemma as they had been praying for us and following our newsletters. Would we be willing to come as candidates for the pastor's job at their church? It was an inner-city church in an African-American community, and they had been without a pastor for two years. Perhaps our experience in Africa would help in understanding the community, and we could build the church up again.

It was worth a look. So, Dick and I went for the traditional candidating for the position of pastor at Central Baptist Church in Sacramento. After our time visiting there, we were very pleased with the prospects, and we waited to see what the church would decide. The vote was *yes* and plans were made that we would move to Sacramento two weeks after the birth of our baby. Little did they know what novices they were getting!

At that time we looked for housing, but returned to Santa Cruz with no success. We sent in our resignation to the mission and began packing our few possessions in preparation to move. After Julie, our delightful little eight-pound four-ounce baby was born, Dick left us (still in the hospital) and traveled to Sacramento where he began looking seriously for a house. He found one, and with Dad Otto's help, he bought it! How do you like that! Sight unseen, I had a house. One beautiful thing about our marriage was that we had come to know each other and our desires so well that I could be fully confident Dick would pick a house with lots of windows, and I would love it. My mother came from Colorado to help us pack and move. When Julie was two weeks old, we moved to our new home in Sacramento.

****

It was in our new church in Sacramento that we discovered some of the reasons why God had allowed Idi Amin to deport us. Did we really think this was not part of God's plan? God can even use a wicked man like Idi to accomplish His will for His children's lives. And indeed, this is exactly what God was doing. By now Dick had resolved his anger, and I was excited about the new doors being opened to us. But as the five years at Central progressed we learned many, many reasons why we were in Sacramento.

In this very church God had placed two men that not only understood discipleship completely, but practiced it. Bill Heyenbruch was the teacher of this basic concept and slowly began teaching Dick. Soon they included two others and they were a team of four. These men met weekly to check on each other and see if they were indeed discipling someone. Bill provided materials that were transferable concepts, and Dick loved it. With the weekly meetings, Dick was learning more and more and men were coming into the church. Two other men joined, and the team was accomplishing great things for God.

Meanwhile, the church was bearing with a very green pastor. Each week precious ladies would encourage or correct their pastor. Oh, the patience these ladies possessed! But I could see that Dick was growing by leaps and bounds! He would choose a book of the Bible and systematically go through that book week by week. Denver Seminary had taught him lots, and one thing was the value of expository preaching. That just simply means that you don't jump around teaching on topics, but you expose a whole book, week by week. It always amazed me how the passage for the week was exactly the passage needed for the problems that the church was facing at the time. I was growing and seeing God's word as a whole. The people in the church were also showing great appreciation for Dick's presentations and growth.

This so inspired me that I wrote a children's curriculum for Children's Church that would take a child through the entire Bible if they were in the program for six years. This was an exciting project for me and gave the teachers in Children's Church continuity to their teaching. It stretched me to find games, activities, and songs to go with each Bible story.

God knew both Dick and I needed all this preparation for the years ahead. I was working with the Children's Church and in the music department. We found musicals that the children could perform. Again my knowledge was being expanded and God was opening up a whole new area of ministry.

Discipleship was happening. Two of the men on the core team decided that if Dick could be in ministry, they could too. Dick was just a common ordinary person, and if God could use him, certainly God could also use them. They both quit their jobs and went off to Denver Seminary. After Jack Bernard finished his work at Denver, he served in Belize as a missionary, as area director for Conservative Baptist Home Mission Society (Now Mission to the Americas) in the Northwest, and finally is ministering in an inner-city church in San Francisco. Steve Reed is serving with Missions to the Americas in Central America. And Dick Otto? By becoming a pastor, and a man of the Word, he was better able to communicate God's Word. He saw people not only come to the Savior, but grow deeply in His Word as a result of his ministry.

Our time at Central was wonderful. We learned to love many people and had faithful friends there. They continued to be patient with us and tenderly teach us God's work of being a pastor.

But after five years, God chose to move us on. Oh, the tears that were shed! I have to say that I *never* liked leaving a place. I was always so happy and could see more things that needed to be done before I could go. I hated leaving friends; it was with much kicking that I allowed God to move us.

"Ivy, I know that with time you will learn to love Oroville," said Dick persuasively.

"But why do we have to move now? The women here are so close to me, and we are having such a good time! They are growing. My friend Elle, from the P.T.A., was just saved! She will need to be discipled and . . . "

"I really feel God wants us to move and start a new church."

"But how will we be supported? Until we get a church started we'll have no money, and I don't think my substitute teaching will bring in enough for us to live on. I hate to see Nancy have to adjust to a new place all over again! It is so hard for her to meet new people, and then Tim has just . . . "

"Honey, I know all that. It is God who wants us to move, not me. And He will make a way. Doesn't He always meet all our needs?"

"Yes," I sighed. "I know all that. It is true. But I just love it here so much! It's so hard to leave people you love. It seems we have to do it so often!"

"Maybe even that is part of God's plan for us . . . learning to leave. You can come back to Sacramento as often as you like to visit. We are only seventy miles away!"

So once again we packed our things. This time the packing was much more difficult than in Uganda! We had acquired so many things, piles and piles of things! I'm still not sure how that happens! We always seem to need more things, but we have so many already, we can't begin to move all of them! Oh well, it was accomplished!

****

Now we were in Oroville. It is just as hot in the summer there as in Sacramento. And this time our move was not in November, as it had been so many times before, but in August—August and September being the hottest time of the year. Would you believe, 112 degrees! No, I think it even got to 122 one day!

How did we find a support system? We had known that our Conservative Baptist Home Mission Society had a section in it called New Churches Now. We wrote CBHMS to see if we could be appointed with them. We told them we felt God had called us to start a church in Oroville, and already another couple wanted to work with us. CBHMS presented to us a three-year program on a descending pay scale. We would have to raise 50% of our total support. The first six months we would receive 100%. Thereafter each six months we would receive fifteen percent less with the church picking up that fifteen percent. Finally, the church would take over the full support. Now we were missionaries with our home society.

God gave us *two* precious couples to work with. John and Sandie Johnson had served with CBFMS (now called CBInternational) in the Ivory Coast. But due to sickness of Sandie's mother, they had returned home. They had three darling daughters. Originally they were the couple that asked us to come and work with them to start a church. The other couple, Bob and Kathy Mills, had three striking sons! We had a son, a daughter, and our little jewel, Julie, by now five years old.

We began with Bible studies in our home. In November we felt that enough people were coming to have our first Sunday worship service. With just the three families we were a healthy fifteen people and we hoped others would also join us. I would work with the youth, Dick the adults, and Nancy would teach the children.

****

One Friday, Elle, our friend from P.T.A. in Sacramento, came to visit us. Elle had come to the Lord after Dick and I made friends with her family. We had witnessed to each of them—especially the husband. The man was greatly overwrought, and Dick had been counseling him. But on Father's day, shortly before we left in August, Elle's husband committed suicide. What a disaster. But, because of it we had grown very, very close to Elle and loved seeing her grow in the Lord. It was good to see her again to have some times of prayer, talk, and fun. When she was about to leave, Dick decided to carry her down the front steps. Remember, I told you Dick has a sense of humor. He is always full of fun and goofing around! Elle was screaming all the way but loving it! Oh, no! On the fourth step from the bottom, Dick slipped and dropped Elle, going down hard on his knee.

"Elle, are you okay?" he shouted, holding his knee and hardly able to breathe! "Don't worry about me!" he managed to mutter.

"My rear hurts, thanks to you! But you don't look too good. Dick, what has happened to you? Oh, please, don't pass out!"

By this time, I was down the steps trying to help Dick sit up.

"Really, I'm OK. You go on home because I know it is late," Dick said to Elle. "Ivy will take me to the hospital. I think the knee I crushed in Colorado back in 1972 has just bent backward. I'll just go to the hospital, they will put it back in place, and I'll be fine."

Reluctantly Elle left. I got the car and took Dick to the emergency room at the hospital.

"Well, tell me, what's happened?" asked the doctor.

"You see Doc, I crushed my left knee back about seven years ago. They pulled the muscles together and sewed them there to replace the kneecap. I think the knee has just bent backward. I'm sure you can fix it."

"Yes, I'm sure we can, but you said that was the left knee?"

"Yes."

"Well, this happens to be your right knee!"

Dick underwent surgery, where they took out three-fourths of the kneecap and left one-fourth to build on. He was in a cast the first Sunday of worship at our house. He sat in a chair and preached! To this day, Dick says that his children built that church, not us! We actually both know that God is the one that built the church, but He did use Tim and Nancy to bring in the youth, and Julie to bring in the children. The children loved Nancy, their teacher, and soon dragged their dad's and mom's along; that is the way the church was built. I do think the youth were attracted as well by those two striking teenagers with red hair!

****

Now what was God's plan for us in Oroville? What was He trying to teach us to prepare us for future ministry? Planting a church. Dick knew that he would need to expose himself to the community, so after he was out of the cast and off the crutches, he began farming. No, I really don't mean that the way you think. What he did was to visit three hundred homes every month. By visiting twenty-five homes each day, three days a week in a designated neighborhood, he could easily reach three hundred homes in a month. Then he would begin the cycle at the first homes he had visited to make the rounds again. So in a year's time, he had been to each home twelve times. Living in Oroville for five years allowed him to really get to know these people. Therefore Dick was pastor to many more people than those in the church. Some of the people began coming to the church but many of them did not; however, when they faced a problem—death, sickness, or marriage—they would call "their pastor," even if they never came to the church.

Dick loved doing this. It exposed him to real problems and gave him great contact with non-Christians. He found many illustrations for his sermons and really did keep in touch with the daily needs of the people he met.

Another thing he did was establish four support groups, each with a leader. To these groups he assigned the church attendees. These groups met monthly for the members to get to know one another better and to pray for one another. When they had problems the people were much more prone to call their leader than Dick. This gave these leaders a feeling of real worth and service. They met with Dick on a regular basis for prayer and discussions.

Dick was learning many things that help to plant a church. He was becoming a more loving pastor and more understanding of the real needs of people. He was able to prepare messages that addressed the problems of the average person. God was indeed training his man for a great work.

Although I was developing skills in youth work, women's work, children's work, and as a pastor's wife, I was encountering new problems. God uses the difficult situations in our lives to help us mature. While I found this to be true, I was also learning that in many ways, I was, indeed, weak.

****

Now, in 1996, I have learned that women, as well as men in their early forties, frequently pass through what is commonly called a "mid-life crisis."

I was forty-two. I do not know that my weaknesses can be attributed to that unsettled period of my life; what I do know is that I did not believe, expect, or understand those weaknesses.

I developed a need to "mother" certain people. I would usually pick a young man or woman that had serious problems. As I worked with the youth groups, I found that I was attracted to certain youth and would attach myself to them in an unhealthy way. I didn't know what was happening to me. I just knew I wanted to spend an excessive amount of time with these kids and thought about them way too much. This was only the beginning of a weakness I would take years to overcome.

Nancy was in her early teens. She and I were so much alike that it was scary. I saw things in her that I did not like—because I was seeing me! We were not getting along very well. She was trying things in life Dick and I really didn't want her involved in. Our kids were still very obedient in attending church and helping a great deal. But things were certainly up and down with Nancy.

The sad thing is that indeed Nancy did know which of my buttons to push to get me angry. I'm sure I was still dealing with the anger I learned from my dad in trying to control people. But because I realized that anger was wrong, I would feel guilty and sad when I yelled at Nancy.

I praise God that while we were raising our kids, we prayerfully did the best we knew how. We definitely failed in many ways, but don't ever let the feeling of guilt haunt you. God realized that we do the best we can, and the trials involved in raising children bring us closer to Him. Our children will be held responsible for their actions as they mature, and someday they may fail in the attempt to be the best parents in the world as well! We are all sinners, we all are responsible for our actions, and we each choose what we will do with the circumstances that come our way. But I have to admit that in being a great parent, with Nancy in particular, I was very weak.

Why do I share these areas of weakness with you? Because life is not all good. We each face tests, and we often fail. But God uses these things to prepare us for future work. He can turn the darkest hours into glorious lessons that we will look back upon with joy. My weaknesses did not disappear overnight. I struggled with the "mothering" complex for too long. But now I can help other women with similar problems, and I certainly understand them better than if I had been "perfect." (Which, by the way, none of us are or can be!)

We loved Oroville. We loved the people and the work. I was not thinking of leaving. I had no desire to leave. We hadn't gotten the church building up yet. We had tried to initiate a building program, but nothing was working out. Each week we had to set up our equipment in an apartment building's recreation room, or in the town Grange Hall. And by that very circumstance, we learned which people had a heart of a servant. The team of "servants" grew closer as we worked together.

But the call came.

Kampala Baptist Church in Kampala, Uganda, wanted Dick and Ivy Otto to come to Kampala to pastor the church there. Though I always hate leaving a place, the love I still carried for the work and people in Uganda had never died and this love took control.

I was elated! Dick could not believe that the nationals of Uganda would really want him to come. Back on our knees! Was this really God's call or was it just *our* great desire to return?

Two years before, just after Idi Amin had been chased away from the country and a new president had taken over, some of our Ugandan friends had expressed a desire for us to come back and help with the work. Yes, at the time following Amin's "Eight Year's Reign of Terror!" One friend was Jacques Masiko. Dick had acted as his "uncle" in the early 1970's and found him a wife. When Dick introduced them, Cecilia was living in our servant's quarters and attending school in Kampala. Her father was a pastor in Western Uganda—an older man, well respected in our churches. Jacques through she was a good choice and married her soon after we left the country. You might remember that it was Cecilia that Nancy loved so much. Also it was Cecilia that prayed with us when we were deported. Cecilia and Jacques, had expressed their desire for us to return.

But the time had not been right then. Our church in Oroville was just not well enough established for us to leave. We prayed about going but had no peace. After a month, another letter came saying that we should not come. The country was embroiled in war again, and things were not stable.

Now a much more official call had come. The country seemed to be settled again. Milton Obote had returned. With the help of the Tanzanian government, Obote took over the country for the second time. Kampala Baptist Church was calling us to come as pastor. When we approached God from the kneeling position, He affirmed that call. By now the church in Oroville was much more settled and had good leadership. We had been working with a young man that could take over as pastor.

We wanted to go as quickly as possible, so we contacted our mission to see if we could go with the MAC program. (Missionary Assistance Core) We were approved. The principal from Lincoln International School called and asked if I would be able to teach. We contacted a few churches that had previously contributed to our support, and they agreed to do so again. In just four months we were ready to go.

The big heartache we faced now was leaving Tim in America. He wanted so badly to go back to Uganda with us, and had begged us to go two years before. Now he had completed high school. He would not be able to go to Rift Valley Academy—the school he had visited when in third grade and had dreamed of attending. We would have to leave him in America.

Tim had been the delight of our life. He had always gotten top grades in school, had been in numerous speech contests from the time he was in seventh grade, and had a cupboard full of trophies to show for his efforts. He had been in the band and performed many times. He and I played trumpet duets. He always had a positive attitude and was a great asset to ministry. In his senior year at Oroville High School he had been student body president and received numerous awards at graduation. Now how could we leave this one behind—this son who was such a great encouragement to us?

In his usual manner, Tim assured us that God would take care of him. He had applied to Biola University in La Mirada, California, and had been accepted. This was his dad's alma mater, and he was excited about going. He reasoned that he would be leaving us anyway. As it turned out, we left before he did. He had two days in Oroville alone, finishing the packing up of the house. I have often had nightmares about how Tim *really* felt about this. Had it broken his heart? Did he feel abandoned? Did he have memories that would be deeply hurtful for years to come? I have never really talked to him about this, but I would like to.

I feel that neglecting to talk about it, or at least to express to Tim my concern, was another serious weakness. In the excitement of going, I was not aware how Tim felt deep down. He assured me that he would be okay. I guess we always carry regrets with us, and sometimes we never learn the whole story.

But we were also anxious about Nancy going to RVA (Rift Valley Academy) in Kenya. She would be in Africa with us, but gone to boarding school three months out of every four. Would she adjust? Would *we* adjust to her being gone from us? Tim was scheduled to leave home for college, but Nancy was only a sophomore in high school! Could we face this with such little preparation? Could she? (She and I still were having some conflicts caused by our similar personalities.) Was my weakness in not fully trusting God showing again? God knew every circumstance of our family. Had He made a wrong decision? Why my faith would waver so often, I don't understand. So many other weaknesses—guilt feelings and my inability to fully commit my children to the Lord—were showing. God would have to continue patiently teaching me. Oh, how good God is!

Although Nancy and I had our problems, this girl was also a delight. First of all, she was beautiful with her golden-red hair. She was vivacious and full of life and excitement. She was a gifted athlete and always involved in something. She did keep the youth in the church alive and was always looking for things to do that would excite them. She led them as they taught at the "Snoopy Day Camp" we had, as they participated in making the props and equipment for all the programs we put on. Nancy was creative and enjoyed working with kids. With Nancy there was never a dull moment, and I knew we would miss her much more than she would ever imagine. While in Oroville, Dick had baptized his "sweet girl" at our church camp. He did it in the swimming pool and still remembers the joy of seeing our girl committed to following Jesus.

Again we had to trust all of this to the Savior. It was Him calling us. He would see us through. Our prayer was that she too would adjust and enjoy being a part of what God had planned for our family. God never calls just the parents; He calls the children as well.

Weaknesses. Hard to face . . . hard to admit. They were many. However, God was still at work in our lives—particularly mine.

CHAPTER 15 – WAR IN UGANDA

"For when I am weak, then I am strong."
-2 Corinthians 12:10b

Nancy and I flew to Nairobi, Kenya, so we could travel the 40 miles to the school, and Dick and Julie into Uganda. Julie had asked me about two months earlier what Uganda was like.

"Mommy, you, Nancy, Tim and Daddy Have all been to Uganda. Tell me what it is like."

"Well Julie, it is . . . different"

"No, I want to know what it is like."

"That is very hard to explain. There isn't too much here in America to compare it to, so I don't know how to explain."

"Well, try!"

Julie had just finished third grade and would be going into the fourth. Since I would be teaching at Lincoln International School where they were sixty-four students, grades kindergarten through sixth, I would be her teacher.

"Well, some of the houses are like the ones here, and some are made of mud. Many are small, and others are big. We will have a house like we have here with a big yard. We won't be shopping in stores like we do here. They do have what they call a "supermarket," but it is very different. We will buy all of our vegetables and fruits at an open market."

"What is an open market?"

"One that is outside. At the outside market you also buy all your dishes, pots, pans, and buckets. The roads are paved, but you drive on the left side of the street instead of the right. That means that the driver's seat is on the right instead of the left as in our car. The schools have hundreds of kids but you will be in a small American school, and that will be . . . well, it will be different too."

"Mommy, you keep saying it is different."

"Yes, let's leave it at that. When you get there, you'll see."

It was fortunate that she was willing to stop there. Just three months later I asked her, "Julie, what is Uganda like? What would you tell your friends in America?"

"Well . . . you are right, Mommy. It is different!"

She now realized why it was so hard to explain. Julie was very special to us. She had a loving, compliant spirit. She was doing well in school and if you gave her a hard look, she would break down in tears. We were happy we didn't have to look forward to losing her just yet. We would have at least two years together, and then we planned to return to America anyway.

I went to Kenya with Nancy and waited the week before RVA started. I roomed in a guesthouse with Nancy and helped her put labels on her clothes. This was a requirement at the school as fewer things were lost in the laundry when they were labeled. I was pleased to accompany her to the school and make sure she was settled in.

When we entered the office to register, I was surprised to see a long time friend, Naomi Kaufman, standing there! I was delighted! She was there with her son, Steve. He was also entering RVA as a sophomore.

Nancy, I want you to meet Steve. He was the boy you played with every day when we were in language school in Kenya back in 1970. You two could hardly be separated!"

"Mother!"

You can imagine the embarrassment she felt. Naomi and I just laughed while Steve made a weak effort to say hello, and Nancy returned the greeting in like fashion. I might add that although it was a terrible introduction, Nancy and Steve became like brother and sister the three years they were together at RVA.

****

When I arrived in Uganda, I found Julie had been a very unhappy girl. She had cried every day at school and every night at home. She was not the adventurous type and being away from Mom coupled with strange surroundings and a new school had almost been her undoing. Julie *never* stayed overnight with friends. It was just too scary. She had always been very close to us and wanted to keep it that way. Julie was joyful when Mom came home and we went to school together.

Uganda did not resemble the place I had feebly tried to describe to Julie. The war had left Uganda so devastated that I cried for months. When we went to town to shop, we would look in the shop windows. If we would see a can of margarine, a bottle of shoe polish, a roll of toilet paper, and a book, we would think that was what was sold in the store. But we would enter to find broken and completely empty shelves. The five items in the window were *all* they had. The open market was the only place that things seemed to be as they were before.

The roads had so many potholes that 60% of them were totally impassable. And the 40% that could be used were so bad you could drive only about ten miles an hour. I was also wrong about driving on the left side of the street. People now drove on the *best* side of the street. There was very little traffic because the roads were so bad. You could almost walk faster than ride. Besides, cars were stolen so frequently that most people didn't want to chance their car being stolen.

The spirit of the people was also broken. Obote, the man that had demoralized them for years, killed many of the Baganda, and ruled with little concern, was back in power. He was calling back the Asians that Amin had chased away. These people were claiming the properties they had owned, so many Ugandans were now homeless. The Asian people ran the shops and treated the Ugandans like dirt.

At least Lincoln International School was a bright spot. We had sixty-four exciting young children. I taught fourth, fifth, and sixth-grade social studies. I also taught some music, art, and drama. Each class had only about eight students, so the teaching was easy and lots of fun.

Another great place was the church. The congregation of Kampala Baptist Church was still meeting at St. John's Ambulance Center. We had Bible study classes before the church time and this was a great attraction to the community. Most churches had Sunday school only for children. Here at Kampala Baptist, university students could come to study the Bible in depth. The church membership numbered about seventy-five, but when the preaching was done on a regular schedule, and the music improved, more and more people started coming and soon attendance was up to about 150 people.

We came back to Uganda with very few things. I did not bring any of my musical instruments, but I was teaching music at Lincoln School and certainly wanted some type of music at the church. We had an excellent guitarist there but no piano or other instruments. One day at the church, I met a young man that had a very small accordion. It had four base notes on it, so it could be played in only two keys.

"Tamali, could I borrow your accordion sometime so I could use it at school?"

"Of course you can. I have another one at home which is much bigger, but it doesn't work."

"What's wrong with it?

"When you try to play, almost all the notes sound at the same time. It just makes noise, not music."

"Well, perhaps it can be fixed."

"You can try. I'll tell you what. I need this accordion Monday night, but then I won't need it again until Sunday. Why don't you send Dick by on Tuesday, and I will give both of them to him for you to use."

I was not prepared for what Dick brought home from Tamali's. The big accordion that did not work was the very same accordion that I lost in Uganda ten years before! Dick and I took it apart to see what could be done to make it work. To our surprise, it was full of cockroaches! They were plugging some holes in the accordion. The accordion is designed with holes for the air to pass through. This is what makes the sound. Other holes were being held open by these invading cockroaches. We sprayed it thoroughly and even found the queen cockroach and killed her. After three days of spraying and chasing cockroaches, we had them all out . . . all 150 of them! We then put new cloth in place of the chewed, and wonder of wonders, it worked!

****

Nancy had love/hate feelings for RVA. She loved the friends, the excitement of the sports, and the joy of being with those friends all the time—day and night. But she hated the rules (which sometimes I too thought were a bit too severe). She hated being away from her family, and she hated the intense effect that a misfortune suffered by one student had on everyone at school. Living in Africa brings many experiences that those in America could not understand—death from stray bullets or soldiers, death from wild animals, sicknesses such as malaria, cholera, or hepatitis. She wanted to go home to America. She spent much of her time, one month out of four at home with us. Each time she begged us to send her to Grandma Otto and let her go to school in California. We just could not bear to send her that far from us. We had a hard time understanding her desire to go to America, for when we would take her back to school, she would not even take time to say goodbye to us in her excitement about seeing her friends and getting back to school. Today she says she would not exchange her three years there for anything! But I regret the weakness I had in not discussing the situation thoroughly with her so she'd have felt more secure in our love.

Julie was having a great time. Mom was her teacher; she had lots of muzungu (white) friends, and had the joy of being with loving Ugandans. She learned how to serve tea when people came to visit. If Mom and Dad were gone and she was alone, she would simply invite the guests in, ask Debra, our house-girl, to prepare tea, and Julie would sit and talk to the guests. We soon found out that people didn't even mind if we weren't at home when they came. They enjoyed being with Julie. It was rare for them to see a young girl that could converse so well and entertain her guests. We were told about their admiration three years later when we were about to return to America.

"We know you missionaries are paid to work with us and do your job, so we aren't sure if you like us or not. But when we see that your children like us and treat us so well, we feel you must be teaching them your values, and so we know you also love us."

Pastor John Ekudu was speaking of Julie. Once again we realized our children had a valid and important part of our ministry.

****

Two years. That was all the time we had committed ourselves to be in Uganda with our MAC program. But the church was growing, the work was satisfying, and the church hadn't been constructed yet. The members had finally, after a very long struggle, purchased land and the building materials were on their way. Nancy had only her senior year left. If we returned to the states, she would be in a new school and have many adjustments to go through again. Although Nancy kept saying that she wanted to go back to America, we knew her well enough to know it would be a very difficult adjustment for her.

With lots of prayer about these considerations, we wrote to Wheaton, Illinois, our home office, to see if they would allow us to stay one more year. It was granted. This was June 1985.

At that time our team consisted of Jack Smith, a single missionary that had come to Uganda just one year before we did and lived next door to us; Sharon Winslow, a single gal that lived next door to Jack; Brent Slater, another single fellow who was ministering in Kasese, about 25- miles west of us; and Fred and Carol Lewis, also in Kasese. Another couple, Skip and Ruth Sorensen, had been appointed to Uganda and were in Kenya in language study. There was also another MAC couple, the Drakes, with their three boys. The picture shows only part of that team.

****

Nancy came home at the end of July to stay through August. We enjoyed having her around. When she was home we usually tried to find some project the girls could do to earn a little money and have a few responsibilities. They might paint the house, make a tire rim basketball hoop, or do some shopping for Mom. Nancy could drive the motorcycle we had and often would take off with Julie on the back. There was lots of excitement and fun when she was at home.

****

Saturday, July 29th, I was finishing up a wedding cake that was to be delivered Sunday afternoon.

"Oh, no, we missed it! I wanted to learn how to make the flowers for the cake. I also wanted to see how you put the cake together. When will we be able to come again?" said one of the ladies wanting to learn how to make wedding cakes.

"Well, I did tell you to come on "muzungu" time, not African! Sorry, I had to finish up as I have another appointment this afternoon. I will be making another wedding cake next month. I'll be sure to let you know when we do so you can see it all. But come, watch me put the leaves on and these last frills."

As the four of us gathered around the four-tier cake with two large cakes shaped like a Bible in front, we heard three loud explosions. These ladies had lived in Uganda all their lives and those sounds were no mystery to them. One lady exclaimed, "Oh God! The children are at home alone!" Then I knew . . . those were guns . . . no, actually cannons! My husband and Julie had just left the house two minutes before on the motorcycle. I felt a sick faintly feeling in my stomach; I too prayed.

"Oh, God, what defense will they have on a motorcycle? Please, protect them and help them find a safe place!"

My three guests had no hesitation in finding an inner storage room in the center of the house. They entered it and sat on the floor. They had with them a three-week-old baby and a ten-year-old girl. All of them were crying.

The guns, rocket launcher, and cannons were close. We knew this was the rumor come true. For two weeks we had heard that part of the army had rebelled against Obote and was taking over parts of Uganda, but we never dreamed they would be in Kampala so soon.

After about thirty minutes of heavy gunfire and cannons, it subside a bit, and Dick and Julie came in the front door. Oh, the joy to see them!

"Sorry, Honey," said Dick. "We have been next door all the time. The cannon was just ahead of us, so we turned around immediately and drove into the garage and hit the floor. Jack saw us, grabbed Julie—carrying her into his house—with me close behind. We have been on the floor at Jack's."

The local radio soon announced the takeover and invited the people to the city center to celebrate. So again we heard gunfire that spoke of celebration. It continued for about seven hours, but knowing it was an expression of victory, we were less tense; however, at dark it all got going again and continued for about eight more hours. I'm sure a million dollars worth of ammunition was used in that time. In my wildest imagination I could not believe there was that much ammunition in the whole world, let alone poor, little Uganda! And there is absolutely *no way* I can explain to you what took place the next sixty- four hours. The continual sounds of guns, cannons, machine guns, and rocket launchers could be heard for twenty-four hours with *no* break. We felt that this was no longer celebration but looting! There was about two hours of intermittent firing from 4:00 A.M. to 6:00 A.M. but then it began again. Some was far away, others nearby; and during the sixty- four hours, the longest time of silence we recorded was two minutes!

As we had fearfully suspected, looters—our wonderful new army men—were responsible for many hours of gunfire. Shops, homes, neighbors were looted. Some people were killed, but the gunfire was used mainly just to scare people away so they could loot more freely.

On Sunday people were told to stay at home. No one was to go out. That afternoon we heard three terrific explosions. The army was destroying Obote's house that was just one-half block away from ours. It was Monday morning at 4:00 before the soldiers were finally tired and drunk enough to sleep. Now, we also could get a little sleep.

Sharon, the first term missionary working with university students, moved in with us (she lived in the apartment next to Jack!) We all ate our meals together. On Saturday, the day of the takeover, the Drakes had gone to the American Club on the other side of town to swim. They were caught there and had to stay in the guest rooms at the club. At least they had a phone and were able to contact and keep in touch with us. The Southern Baptist Missionaries were all in Kenya at their annual meetings. They called us many times to check on how things were.

Meals? Well that is an interesting story. Dick had just purchased six chickens on Friday. These were frozen and to be eaten only on special occasions. (At $6 a chicken, they were a real treat.) We all pooled our food. We had cabbage, a few beans, rice, and some potatoes in addition to our chickens. My girls cheered when the cabbage was gone, but soon they were tired of chicken . . . fried, chicken and dumplings, curry, roasted, leftover chicken.

We were worried about our Ugandan friends. They bought food daily. By Wednesday four days had passed with no one able to go out. People were desperate, so quietly they began to send one member of the family out to look for food. Shops that had now been looted had some food, but the prices were double! The little food at the open market was also priced astronomically. Some of our friends found their way to our house, so with the added mouths to feed, it didn't take long until both our rice and beans were also gone.

And what was happening day by day? It amazes me how immobile war makes you. I started this book way back then. But I absolutely could not concentrate on it for even one minute. My eyes would see the words but not comprehend the meaning. I could not write letters because my thoughts were so disconnected. Cooking was the easiest task we had, but we were running out of things to cook. Games, yes, we forced ourselves to play games just to pass the time of day.

One day when Jim Rice called from Kenya where the Southern Baptists were meeting, we begged him, "Pray!" For about two hours previous to his call we sat and listened to a looter's truck on the block behind us. It would drive into a yard. Then we would hear gunshots. We assumed the looters were probably blowing off locks and warning the people to keep out of their way. Then for about ten to twenty minutes we would hear intermittent shouts. Again, the engine would start, the truck would move on down the street to enter another yard. Again the gunshots and shouting. This had taken place at, at least six homes. The truck was rounding the corner just as Jim called. God answered our prayers because the truck turned left—away from our home.

On Thursday, Jack and Dick ventured out to check on Deo, one of our closest friends. We four girls, Sharon, Julie, Nancy and I, had gone to the backyard to play a bit of basketball. By now things were a little quieter. We played for a while, but we lost interest even in that, especially when we heard gunshots just a block away. I was determined that we do something. Just to sit was driving everyone crazy. Being alone without the men was a bit unnerving. But not knowing what action to take, we sat down to play cards. After a short time, the inevitable occurred. Three gunshots at our gate! The warning. We rushed into the back bedroom, which was the most secure in the house, and fell on our knees around the bed. As we prayed, God gave me an idea. If I opened the door and allowed them in, perhaps the locks would not be destroyed and they would be more relaxed as they did their work.

"Girls, pray. I am going to go open the front door for them."

I unlocked the door, opened it, and saw no one—at least at the door. I cautiously stepped out. Coming up the sidewalk were Jack and Dick. I almost collapsed! Had they seen the looters at our gate? Where had they gone? Dick and Jack said they had heard some gunshots that were very close as they neared our street. But when they turned up the street that led to our home, they only saw one lone soldier walking quickly up the street. Perhaps he had seen the men around the corner and decided that since he was alone, he would not loot our place.

The army put a roadblock on our street right at our gate. The soldiers would arrive about dark to stop cars and people from going towards Obote's house. On Thursday evening, when the shooting began again, Nancy went into hysterics. She came into our room crying that she could take no more. She was going to run away! Both Dick and I had to grab her and force her into bed with us to keep her from going. She was so scared she was not making any sense. Julie was awake by now. She was losing weight. We knew we would have to do something to save our girls.

Friday we contacted the Drakes—still at the American Club. Did they think they could get to their house to pack a few things? Yes, most of the people caught at the club had gone home the day before. We then laid plans for their car and ours to go by convoy out of Kampala toward the border. We knew that the borders were closed but we would attempt to go into Kenya at all cost. We planned to leave at 6:00 Saturday morning since we knew that would be the quietest time. We prayed we would be able to go into Kenya about 150 miles from Kampala. Jack would be our contact in Kampala. I think he felt safe enough, and things were quieting down a bit. He would try to keep our three houses safe. Sharon went with us.

We were packed and ready to leave. At 6:00 A.M. the Drakes drove into our yard. As soon as they arrived we piled into our car and followed them out the front gate. The soldiers, to whom we had talked and told we were leaving, were sound asleep. We drove out of town. About thirty minutes later the sun began to rise; we saw no armed men and heard no gunshots. In fact, as we drove the four hours to the border, we saw people walking on the road, merchants selling their wares. It seemed as if there was no war at all! Then over the car radio, at about 8:10 A.M. we heard this announcement:

"President Okello, the new president of Uganda is happy to announce that because his coup was successful, he has opened the borders to Zaire, Rwanda, Sudan, and Kenya."

What joy! What relief! We were the first two cars at the border! And just behind us was a friend. What a story he had! He was at work the Saturday the coup occurred, in the same building as Obote's offices. The army was looting, breaking things, and arresting every person they met in that building. So Robert, an Asian, hid in the restroom! He stayed there the entire week! During the previous night he had slipped out of the building, found his car, and driven as fast as he could for the border, where we met him!

We drove on to Kisumu, Kenya, which is on Lake Victoria, the second largest lake in the world. Here we found a hotel, ate, and rested. What beautiful rest! There is no way to explain the relief we felt. We shed tears of joy over how God had been with us, protected, and blessed us. What precious fellowship we had there.

Missionaries from our mission were in the states. Their home in Mombasa, Kenya, was vacant. We were told that we could stay there until we felt it was safe to return to Uganda. We welcomed the invitation.

Nancy had wanted me to make a formal dress for a special banquet she would attend at her school, Rift Valley Academy. With time on my hands, I borrowed a sewing machine from another fellow missionary, and was able to make her dress. That filled most of the three weeks we stayed there. We did do some swimming in the Indian Ocean and relaxed a bit. But we were anxious to return to Uganda. After the three weeks, Nancy returned to school; Dick, Julie and I returned to Uganda.

****

I wish I could say that Okello had taken over in order to eliminate the oppression of Obote, or that he had the interests of the people at heart. I am sad to say neither was true. Okello was an elderly man who allowed his army to "do as every man deemed to be right in his own eyes" (Judges 21:25). I call it the six-month "reign of terror." Perhaps the real reign of terror had been with Idi Amin; I was not in Uganda to live through that. But I was present in July of 1985 and the months following. At Lincoln School where I taught, we made plans for housing the students in case war came; we located the safest places in the school for shelter, and we had each student bring blankets and canned foods in case we would be stranded there for a while.

The army continued to loot shops and homes. In fact, after a couple of months, they began writing letters to communities to expect them. "Collect your things together," they would write, "We will be there this evening to pick them up!"

Frequently cars were taken at gunpoint. As Julie and I were leaving school one day, thieves stopped us and ordered us out of the car. It happened that the car's battery had been dead, and I had to push start it before I could go to pick up Julie. So I turned off the key, and asked permission to get my books out of the back seat. Julie had jumped out her door and was screaming wildly, "Run, Mom. Run! Forget your books!" She was very scared. The thieves were waving their guns at the on-coming cars, ordering them to stop. They jumped in the car, but it would not start. I told them it had to be pushed. By now crowds were gathering but were very fearful of the waving guns. The thieves finally realized the car would not start, and jumped into their own car to make their getaway. The crowds dispersed, Julie and I got in the car and someone from the school helped push us to start. Julie and I drove back into the schoolyard to gain control of our emotions. We cried on the shoulders of the other teachers to get rid of the tension! I calmed Julie down and once again after a push start, drove home to tell the story to my husband.

It was only a few weeks later that Dick met a friend at the borders of Kenya and Uganda to pick up a heavy load of steel joints for the church we were building. He had driven the 125 miles from the border and was just one block away from the church site where he was to deliver the joints when a car pulled in front of him, men jumped out of it and ordered him out of the car at gunpoint. Dick stood and watched the car being driven away by thieves. This time God was merciful. Another car that had been stolen and recovered had the steel joints in its trunk! So, we recovered most of the materials for the church. Two months later, the police called and said that they had recovered our car.

"We advise you not to drive the car," they told us.

When we inquired why not, this is the story that we were told.

After the police had spotted the car and taken it (also at gunpoint), they "used" it for a few days. While they were driving it, thieves tried to steal it again, and there was a shootout. One policeman was killed, and some of the thieves were captured. The police felt that our car was "hot" and the thieves would be back to try to steal it again.

The car sat in our yard for another month—with the broken windows that had been shot out. We decided to paint a blue line on the car to mark it very plainly. Our Datsun was once one of hundreds, but with the painted stripe down its side, it was now one of a kind.

****

Though stress was building, our confidence was in the Lord. Dad Otto and Tim, our son, came to Uganda during this time to help work on the church. Dad is an excellent carpenter and a contractor. His expertise was needed to do all the finishing work. Tim was willing to do whatever was needed. Tim was now a junior at Biola and intended to return to the states in February. He was to report to Washington D.C. where he would do a term working with the government. This was in partial fulfillment of one of his college courses. He had decided to join his grandpa, help work on the church, be with his family for Christmas, and then return to D.C.

We had a wonderful Christmas. The church was taking shape. The Ugandans enjoyed Dick's dad and were excited when Tim was around. Tim did magic tricks and he infatuated the kids and youth with his act. He soon had many followers and friends. He used the magic to present the gospel. We were thrilled when he was invited to one of the big schools in the area to give his presentation at an assembly.

****

On January 24th, 1986, we heard them coming. I was at school. For the last four days we had heard the fighting, the airplanes, and the approaching war. Up to then the fighting was taking place about ten miles out of Kampala. Mom Otto had called and pled with Dad to take a plane out. We tried to get him on the evacuation plane but were unable to do so due to roadblocks. When the people continued to flee into the capital and report that Museveni, the leader of these invaders, was just five miles out of the city, the teachers called parents and evacuated the children to their own homes. The children whose parents could not be reached were sent home with friends, or the teachers themselves took the children home. Julie and I rushed home and thankfully found that Dad and Tim had come home from the church with Dick and were waiting for us.

This time was different—it was a real war, not just a military take over! People were actually fighting each other. We could tell where the war was being fought by the location of the sounds of fighting. On top of Kololo Hill, where we live, was a large detachment of Okello's soldiers. They were firing a cannon with shells about two feet long and four inches in circumference. (We know, because we later went to the site and collected the empty shells for vases!) The target was across town toward the west from where Museveni was approaching with his army. Our greatest concern was that on the very hill they were firing on, Rubaga, our mission owned a house and one of the couples from the church lived there.

During the next thirty hours, we heard Okello's army retreat and Museveni's army overrun it. Slowly the fighting moved across the city. Only once did we feel we needed to sit on the floor to avoid bullets. Dad and I decided to build a model of the Old Testament tabernacle while this was all going on! Yes, we had brought to Uganda a small model of the tabernacle, which had remained in the cupboard untouched up to now. Because I knew we would not be able to concentrate on anything else, I got it out and we began to work on it.

Soon we heard noises in the yard. When we looked out our windows, we could see Okello's army fleeing down the hill, through yards and on the streets, out the east side of Kampala. We realized the cannons had stopped and the regiment of Okello's army that had been deployed at the top of Kololo was on the retreat. Thankfully Museveni did not have to pass our way. As the fighting continued, he by-passed our hill by going through the valley just one mile below us. About 7:00 the evening of the twenty-fifth, we heard the drums of celebration in the west part of town. The fighting continuing in the east and slowly faded away. Museveni had taken the city; Okello's troops had fled.

During all this time, Nancy had been at RVA hearing the news on the radio and reading newspaper articles about the war. It was extremely hard for her. She remembered the coup and the dread it had brought. I honestly think the war was harder for Nancy than it was for us in Uganda because she did not know the real thing was much quieter than the coup had been. Yes, more people were killed, but there was a purpose to this war. Museveni was fighting for the rights of the people and true freedom from terror!

In the days that followed a peace came over the city that had not been experienced in months. (The dead bodies were picked up as soon as possible.) Museveni threatened to execute soldiers on the spot if he found them looting or doing anything that would hurt the civilians. It only took one such death to convince the army that its general was serious and he would protect the people.

Things did not calm down immediately, but we could feel the peace and freedom of Uganda begin to build once again. Tim was able to fly out in early February and to this day Dad Otto says, "I wouldn't have missed this for anything!" Mom Otto was relieved to know we all were okay, as was Nancy, and Dad went back to work on the construction of the church. The church had seventeen bullet holes through the roof but they were soon repaired and by March, Dad Otto was on his way back to California and Mom.

CHAPTER 16 – REAPPOINTMENT TO AFRICA

"You did not choose me, but I chose you and appointed you to go and bear fruit – fruit that will last."
-John 15:16

No gunshots for a whole night? Impossible? No, it was magnificently true! Museveni brought peace to Uganda—well, at least to Kampala, which is the place that directly involved the Ottos. With peace came celebrations and a sense of liberty.

Now, don't get me wrong. Uganda was not perfect. In life there will always be both good and bad! We still had our thieves. In fact, one day after being in town, we returned home to find thieves had broken into the house and taken the beautiful $800 electric piano that was to go into the new church! I have learned that the good and bad of life may be a test to see where *our* emphasis will be—we can look at the bad side of the circumstance, or we can choose to focus the good. Look, and you will see there are always both sides there!

School was wonderful! We didn't have to think about making it into a bomb shelter. Now we could focus teaching and "funning." My husband says, "If it isn't fun, my wife won't do it. I call her a 'funner.'" Indeed, I do enjoy life—especially the fun things. I had retreats in our home for the students at Lincoln. I would take two or three classes at a time so we would have about twenty-five students. And because Skip Sorensen, our fellow missionary, had a telescope, of course we had to have an all-night party at one of the parent's home located on a hill. What better way to study astronomy than to actually look at the stars and planets?

But as I said, there is always that other side. I was still having my "mothering" problems. At this time I became interested in a young man and then his entire family! Although the Lord was working on this area of my life, I had a long way to go. Life was a bed of roses; complete with the thorns . . . opposites. However, with the country at peace, a delightful job at the school, the joys of pastoring Kampala Baptist Church, and seeing the new church building being completed, things seemed almost perfect.

In July we went to Nancy's graduation from RVA. I had taken pictures of Nancy and sent them to all the relatives announcing her senior year. At the graduation I took enough pictures to paper a wall in the house. Nancy was extremely excited but cried rivers realizing she would soon be leaving all of these deep, deep friendships.

There were eighty-six graduates in that RVA class of 1986. In l996, their ten-year reunion, they decided to meet in Lancaster, Pennsylvania. You must realize that when at RVA, these students came from at least twenty different countries. The majority was from the U.S. and Canada. The remarkable thing was that at the 1996 reunion, sixty-five of the eighty-six graduates were in attendance! Now that is commitment and closeness! I think the kids at RVA develop family-like relationships; they are certainly more than just friends.

****

Our three years were up; it was time for us to return to the U.S. Nancy was going to America to start her university years, Julie would begin junior high, and Tim would be graduating from Biola University the following year. We had good things to look forward to!

God's main goal for me was to conform me to the image of His Son (Romans 8:29), and He was also saying that my attitude should be the same as that of Christ Jesus (Philippians 2:5). He still had a big job ahead . . . but He was making some progress.

****

Our trip home was a delight. We stopped first in Nairobi to attend Nancy's graduation. Then we flew into Italy. That was a step closer to the culture we would experience in the U.S. There we sampled delightful foods that we had not seen for three years. In fact, when we sent Julie to buy apples, she came back with nectarines! We were in Rome for a few days and saw some of the tourist attractions. The traffic was much the same as in Uganda and Nairobi—wild!

Nancy was anxious to return to the U.S. Each evening as we entered our room for a night of rest, we were deluged with "Please, just send me home. Don't spend all this money on me! I just want to go back to America." But the following day she would roam the streets with us, eat lunch at a sidewalk café, look at the phenomenal sights, be harassed by the Italian men, and seemed to enjoy it all, except the men! But each night she begged to go on to the states alone.

We went on to Holland and had the privilege of staying in the home of the Graffs—friends from Sacramento days. From their home, we rode their bikes along the dikes and visited the windmills and wooden shoe shops. Then we flew into Brussels and visited the Hurlburts. They had been our fellow workers in Uganda in 1969. They loaned us their car, and we drove into Germany and toured up the Rhine and saw some of the castles. It was all so delightful and refreshing. The girls and I went back to Holland while Dick flew to London to visit Moses and Rose Ochwo, a very talented Ugandan couple that had been sent to London Bible College for training.

****

Finally we flew back to Ukiah, California. It is located in the Northern part of the states, where Dick's family now resided. According to Nancy, that is where we always should have been! Although just six weeks later she confessed that she had been wrong. She realized the fantastic experiences she had had living in Africa and visiting Europe. She was sharing things in class at Mendocino College that caused the eyes of fellow students to bug out! Indeed she was a privileged individual and was finally realizing it and being thankful.

Julie was being her usual self as well. Each day as Dick walked her to her new school (she was now a big seventh grader), she would cry, but just before she turned to corner to face fellow students, she would wipe the tears away and go on to make new friends. Actually she made friends with little effort, but it always takes time to adjust to new surroundings.

And once again I was off to school. This time I would be teaching sixth, seventh, and eighth graders at Deep Valley Christian School. The classes were small—about eight students each—so the load was light. Except . . . Ugandan children sat on the edge of their seats and feast on every word that comes out of the teacher's mouth! There are no discipline problems and the children are starved to learn . . . music, math, and social studies . . . whatever!

The expatriate children at Lincoln School had few discipline problems. They sometimes challenged what was being done, but they always enjoyed the classes. Paper, supplies, and opportunities were cherished and taken care of.

In America . . . at the Christian school . . . things were *very* different. When I confronted the students about dropping paper on the floor and treading on it because many children in the world didn't even have paper, the reply was, "So what? Send the paper to them, we don't care." And discipline? Well, needless to say, I was in a different world.

But I loved it! Junior high is not only a challenge, but lots of fun. I was asked to be the sponsor for the eighth-grade class. They were looking forward to graduating. I met a delightful couple while planning lots of field trips and exciting times for the eighth graders. Jerry Irwin works for the California Department of Fish and Game and Linda is a homemaker technician. They were often able to adjust their schedule so they could go with us as the parent sponsors on these trips. I will be forever thankful that this was possible, because they are now two of our most delightful friends in the U.S. You need friends at home so you can correspond with them and be encouraged by them.

So many things happened this year and a half in the states. Dick had fallen on a reconstruction job with his Dad and broken two ribs. Although he was back on the job a month later, we were very grateful for my job so we could have food on the table.

Nancy was off to college, however she was frustrated with me. I was teaching full time, trying to be a mother full time, and visiting churches full time. Some of the cooking and home responsibilities were up to her. I think she was also frustrated with herself. She was determined to experience all that she had missed while at RVA. She felt there had been too many rules—which may be true. But she wanted to get into the things of the world. She realized this was wrong and was trying to do these things behind our backs.

Julie was facing a lot of cultural changes. One day when Aunt Chris asked her to babysit and vacuum the house, we got a call.

"Mom," came the tearful voice over the phone, "What is a vacuum? And what did Aunt Chris mean?"

We went immediately to her rescue and taught her one more nicety of America.

****

This was not a bad time, but it was full of pressures and decisions. We had decided that we wanted to go back to Uganda full time with CBInternational. We loved the work there, the challenges, and our feeling of being used of God. It seemed to us that in America the opportunity to learn about God was everywhere. In Uganda, there was little opportunity for people to be trained and learn of God, and so perhaps our gifts would be of greater use there.

In January of 1987 we went to Wheaton, Illinois, our headquarters and once again were appointed with CBInternational (at the time, CBFMS). I realized that "I did not choose Him but He chose me and *appointed* me to go and bear fruit—fruit that will last." (My version of John 15:16). We were appointed with the mission to return to Uganda and serve there—and I prayed—to bear fruit.

We were to visit churches to raise our support. The amount we needed seemed astronomical! But God was able, and we began the task. That is when I was truly doing three full times jobs at once . . . teaching, traveling, and being a wife and mother. I am sure I was doing less than my best at all three.

Nancy and Dick were not satisfied with the time spent with them. My job at the school involved too much work after classes. I would arrive home around 6:30 or 7:00 in the evening. Because we did so much traveling, on Friday I would come home at 5:00 P.M., we would jump in the car and drive 150 miles to a church, speak all weekend, drive back to Ukiah after the service to reach home about 12:00 midnight, and I'd be back at school at 8:00 the next morning. Dick was going wild trying to fill in all the gaps I was missing. He suggested counseling. I was *too* busy!

June 2, 1987, my mother came from Colorado so she could attend Tim's graduation. The first day she was in California, I went off to school. I had the eighth-grade graduation party and ceremony to prepare. Dick and she were going to shop. As Mom walked down the steps at our apartment, she slipped on a step, fell, and broke her hip!

A week later, with Mom still in the hospital, we drove to Los Angeles, about five hundred miles away to attend Tim's graduation. After our full weekend at graduation, I rushed back for the last week of school and to check on Mom. She had done well in surgery and was sent home the day of the eighth-grade graduation. And what a day that was!

At the swim party, I went for a ride on a four-wheeler. During the years I worked at Lincoln School in Uganda, I drove a motorcycle to school nearly every day. Julie rode on the back. I thought this four-wheeler would be easier to drive than the motorcycle. Wrong! Halfway down the road I hit a bump and the wheels turned sharply. I simply did not have the strength to right the wrong. It all happened very quickly. I plowed into a barbed wire fence and flipped the four-wheeler upside down! I didn't even have the sense to turn off the motor! I was a bloody mess . . . I still have the scars!

With my wounds, and my mom at home and needing help, I still had to attend graduation. Julie agreed to stay home with my mom. Dick was very upset about my careless accident, my continual *urgent* work schedule, and my neglect of him and Nancy. I was feeling guilty about my work and seeming disregard of my family. He was feeling so stressed that he felt we needed to go for counseling. He had talked to me about it a couple of months before, but I had refused. I had enough chaos to deal with without adding counseling. I know counseling is *heavy* and I'd have to do a lot of changing!

Things did settle down when school was out. We nursed Mom back to health and put her on a plane back to Colorado. She had enjoyed the time with our family but was happy to go home to her husband—my step-dad. Nancy was much happier now that I was home to cook and be around. Julie was having fun with her newfound friends and summer vacation. Dick thought we still needed to talk to a counselor about the chaos of the year. We agreed to see a counselor in Santa Rosa and began four sessions.

Our time in counseling proved very helpful. I learned that I was a work--aholic, and Dick was the enabler. The work-a-holic idea was not really new to me, but at least it alerted me to the fact that I was one and should seek ways to change it. A greater revelation was Dick had been enabling me to continue being a work-a-holic. This was of great interest to him. He gained new understanding from this time of counseling. Our most important lessons were that counseling could be very helpful. It doesn't necessarily mean you are sick! It means we don't know how to solve all problems on our own, and it is often valuable to seek information from someone else. I think it was this experience that was the door to open up a whole new area of our lives. We learned the value of counseling, saw things that needed work in our lives, and were no longer afraid to seek help when we met an impasse. The time we spent in counseling actually later led us to become counselors ourselves.

CHAPTER 17 - GOD AT WORK IN UGANDA

"Let love and faithfulness never leave you. Bind them around your neck; write them on the tablets of your heart."
-Proverbs 3:3

"Following our counseling we decided that we would spend our full time speaking at churches to raise the support we needed to return to Uganda. Things settled down significantly. The mission was paying us some salary now that they again employed us, so I no longer needed to work at the school. Nancy was off to Biola University, and Julie, finally adjusted to her new school, was a happy eighth grader. In one year's time we had our support and were scheduled to return to Uganda January 1st, 1988.

We had a wonderful time at Christmas with our immediate and extended Otto families! It would be our last time together for about five years and we hoped to make it the best Christmas yet. After the wonderful festivities at Dad and Mom Otto's place with all the relatives—Dick's two brothers, his sister, their families, and the twenty of us—took off for Lake Tahoe and a few days of skiing. It was absolutely beautiful! The snow floated softly down between the pine trees, turning the entire world into a sparkling fairyland of white. Many times I had walked in the woods enjoying such scenes in my past, so it brought back many wonderful memories of how God had led in our lives. Besides all the good Christmas cooking, the fellowship with Dick's crazy brothers—much like Dad and Dick—the skiing also was good!

We were sorrowful to be leaving Tim who was planning to go to Guatemala to learn Spanish. Besides that we were leaving Nancy behind. We knew the financial support we had raised would not be adequate to provide fully for Nancy, and that was very difficult for us. But it would enable us to help her considerably more than we had been able to help Tim. We were thankful for that. Julie would be going back to Africa with us, but she would be off to boarding school at RVA.

I mentioned that it was hard leaving our children. But it was also hard leaving all our friends. In a prayer letter I wrote this poem:

Today I fear a sad day,

As God has asked us to part;
It fills our hearts with sorrow,
And we wonder what life's about.
> We hang our heads so hopelessly,
> As we start to meet the pain;
> And we really wonder if He loves us,
> Or if life will be the same.

But as He calls us onward,
And He really understands;
Don't fall into self-pity,
And miss all of God's plans.
> He really loves us dearly,
> And allowed our paths to cross;
> But now has called us forward,
> And our acquaintance was not a loss.

So, instead of grieving sadly,
Rejoice as we go our way;
And when you're feeling lonely,
Go to Him and pray.
> He had our special meeting,
> That our lives could be enriched;
> But He is really the One,
> To whom we must be hitched.

He has some other people
On ahead and on our way;
Just thank Him for each blessing,
And walk with Him each day.

We flew out of San Francisco to Amsterdam on December 30th. Due to the time change (Europe and Africa are from eight to eleven hours ahead of the U.S. time) our flight from Amsterdam to Nairobi was on December 31st so we celebrated the in-coming New Year on the plane. We landed in Nairobi on the first of January 1988. Can you imagine being in twenty-three degree weather on December 29th, skiing down the slopes, and two days later swimming in a pool in eighty-five-degree weather?

****

We had decided that if we were going to spend the rest of our working days in Africa, we had better learn some of the languages. English is used extensively in Uganda, but most people up-country don't know it. We decided to brush up on our Swahili in Nairobi for three months and then take a stab at learning Luganda when we arrived in Uganda.

I also had a secret reason for wanting to take the three-month Swahili course. The classes would be at the Church Mission Society Guest House in Nairobi, Kenya. Julie was to enter RVA the second day of January. Since RVA is only forty miles from Nairobi, we would be able to check on her about every two weeks if we did the language study in Nairobi. We really didn't know how Julie would adjust to being away from her folks for she had never enjoyed even staying with friends for a night. But again, God was faithful. Julie had witnessed the struggle that Nancy had put herself through, and so she decided she would look for the best parts of RVA. She knew she would be there for the next five years, and she might as well enjoy it. And she did.

After three months of Swahili, it was back to Uganda (and away from Julie). Our nest was indeed empty! We got involved in the Luganda language study and asked two young men to teach us each morning. Then we thought it would be beneficial if they moved in with us so we could practice all the time. We enjoyed them so much; they became a big part of our lives. They were typical youth that enjoyed singing, joking, and general goofing off. Alas! We did most of our communication in English! So much for learning Luganda! And I'm sad to say, one of the young men became the object of my perpetual mothering.

We studied each morning for about a year, trying to learn Luganda. Then we decided it was beyond us and gave it up. I keep trying on a daily basis but still know just basic conversations in Luganda.

During all this time, we were building rich relationships with the Ugandans and really enjoying our work. Dick was mainly into leadership development and church planting. John Ekudu, a young man we had known in 1970, and worked with while Dick pastored Kampala Baptist Church, had wanted Dick to come back as pastor of Kampala Baptist. Dick knew that John was a natural leader and outstanding speaker. Dick refused to be pastor, and so John was forced to take over and was doing an excellent job. Dick continued to be on the board of elders and encourage all the elders and leaders there. The attendance had risen to about 350 since the completion of the new building.

I had been working with the women of KBC and we were having a great time. We had in-depth Bible studies, times of encouraging women in areas they could raise money to support their families, and times of crafts. Although I mainly worked with the children, these women were a challenge and delight to me. We had a special conference at the church and I was delighted with the response of the women.

In 1986 Dr. Rick Goodgame felt a need to begin a work in the Luganda language. He was a professor at the medical school—a missionary with the Southern Baptists. Rick was good at Luganda, and he had started a church service at Kampala Baptist Church. The Luganda service was at 8:00 A.M. and the English/Luganda Sunday School classes at 10:00. English service began at 11:00. Soon attendance at the Luganda service was about 150. Rick left that work to the Ugandan leaders and started a work in his home in Kololo, the area of town we live in.

In fact, the planting of churches in Kampala was reflective of the church planting going on in the entire country. When we returned in 1983, there were about one hundred Baptist churches in Uganda. Now, in 1988, there were about three hundred.

****

One thing in the culture that I have a hard time dealing with is the Ugandan concept of time. If a meeting is to begin at 1:00 P.M., they are on time if they arrive at 2:00 . . . 3:00 . . . 3:30! In the village, you are on time if you arrive within 2 days of the date! I know that these people are relationship and event-oriented, but it does clash with my culture! I was studying the Psalms and was surprised to see that fourteen times God's love and faithfulness was mentioned. Then I continued my study into the book of Proverbs. There again, to my surprise was a command that we were to be loving and faithful. "Let love and faithfulness never leave you. Bind them around your neck, write them on the tablets of your heart." (Proverbs 3:3). God was teaching me that although Ugandans are often late (according to our timing), and sometimes did not even show up, *I* was to remain faithful — and love them in the process. God was so faithful and loving towards me. In our terms it seemed things went so slowly in Uganda but in just five years two hundred new churches had been started!

****

With the tremendous church growth, the Baptist Union of Uganda (BUU) was being strengthened and new national leaders were coming forth. Michael Okwalko was emerging as a leader. Moses Ochwo had come back from London and was now the director of the theological school in Jinja. John Ekudu continued to be a national leader as well as the pastor at Kampala Baptist Church. Jacques Masiko was now the director of Compassion International. The greatest thrill of all for Dick was to see these men come forth as leaders and do things the Ugandan Way.

The church decided to have a Missions Rally on October 9th, 1988. The leaders of BUU and the church were beginning to realize the message of the great commission. We set a goal of raising 600,000/- (Ugandan shillings) to help send out four new missionaries. To gather this type of money, it would mean that six hundred Ugandans would have to give approximately one full week's wages! And to find four capable men to become missionaries, we would have to do a lot of praying!

At the rally we had a mass choir of sixty, invited nine churches, and fed over 650 people. At the call for those willing to serve as missionaries, four came forward! When the offering was counted we had 568,000/-! The faith of the people grew as they realized the many answers to specific prayers.

Meanwhile, I was excited at how God was opening doors for me. After leading children's choirs at Kampala Baptist, and holding overnight retreats for children at the church, I had been asked to be the official Children's Director. In October, just the week after the Missions Rally, the children had presented *Psalty's Heart to Change the World,* a children's musical about missions. At Christmas, they did another Psalty program. Then at Easter time in 1989, we did *To See A Miracle,* and we were asked to present it on the national television station!

Besides the good children's choir presentations there was the Sunday school. I now had a staff of nine Sunday school teachers and each was being trained.

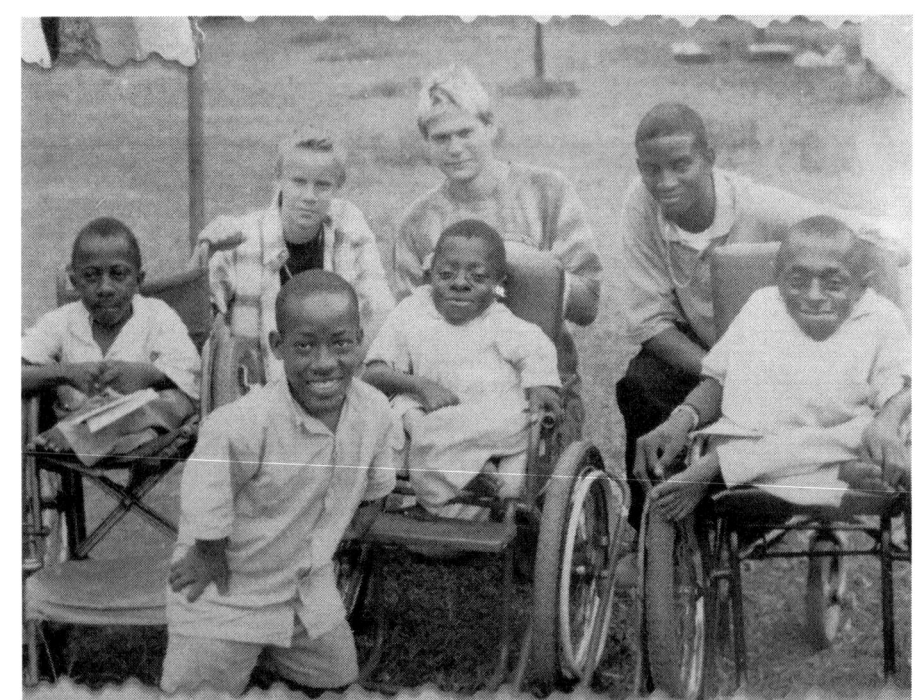

One Sunday we tried to teach the children what it would be like to be handicapped. In Uganda, handicapped people are looked down upon and treated unkindly. In fact, the people are *afraid* of mentally handicapped people. They actually believe the sickness will jump on them if they get too near. We knew we had a great fear to overcome if we expected children to relate to handicapped children. After we tied arms behind backs and asked them to write with their teeth, bound legs up and asked them to run a race, and blindfolded children and told them to simply find a chair and sit, we asked them how they had felt. We got varied answers. Then we said, "Children that are handicapped have the same feelings that you do." The following Saturday we visited the school for the handicapped, saw the work of the children, performed a concert for them, and asked them to join us in singing. We had lunch at the school and our children got to play with these kids— some pushing the wheelchairs. The children grew from this experience and we heard that some began to reprimand parents when they criticized the handicapped people they met.

****

    By 1988 Uganda was facing the greatest handicap of all. In 1983 we had buried Christine, the schoolteacher that had often taken care of Tim and Nancy way back in 1970. She had suffered beyond belief—growing thinner and thinner by the day, developing rashes—and doctors had no idea what she had. But about a year after that, cases like hers were cropping up all over Uganda. The people here began to call it "Slim." America was reporting that homosexuals were also dying of common diseases due to the loss of the protection of their immune systems. It was called HIV (Human Immunodeficiency Virus) and the final states were called AIDS (Acquired Immunity Deficiency Syndrome). Very soon it was realized that the same thing was happening here to heterosexual people.

    By May of 1988, the world knew about the terrible AIDS epidemic in Uganda. Dr. Rick Goodgame, the Southern Baptist doctor, had organized a campaign to educate people in Uganda and bring hope to these people. 20,000 Bibles were distributed along with information about AIDS and God's answer to the problem. The pamphlet explained the truth about AIDS and how, if people would obey the Word of God, they could escape it entirely. The plan of salvation was also presented for all people but particularly to those who had AIDS. It brought the hope of forgiveness and eternal life with the Savior. People handing out the Bibles and pamphlets were available to explain them and to pray with people that wanted to receive the Savior.

People did come to the Lord and a major effort was made to educate people about the disease.

****

While all of these things were happening in Uganda, Julie was thoroughly enjoying school at RVA. She was playing on the volleyball team, learning all about field hockey, meeting kids from twenty-six different nations, and generally talking about all this so much, we chuckled to hear her. Whereas Nancy did little sharing of her school days here in Africa, Julie almost shared too much!

Tim went to Guatemala in February of 1988. He was there for a year. He studied Spanish and visited Nicaragua and El Salvador. These countries reminded him of Uganda and of Belize where he had spent one summer with Jack Bernard, our old friend from Sacramento. His Spanish was greatly improving and he loved the travel and friends he was meeting. He lived with a family in Guatemala and that truly proved to be interesting for him. He learned a lot of the culture living with the people there and did learn to speak their language.

Nancy had transferred from Biola to Sacramento State College, as it was much less expensive. Then joy of joys, she came with Heidi, a girl from Sac State, to Uganda for a visit! She was with us in June and July!

Martin Ssempa, a Ugandan university student, had written a drama called, "*The Cross and the Virus.*" This was another positive effort to educate students about AIDS and to encourage them to not have sex until marriage. The play had four acts and all four acts brought both tears and laughter from the audience. Nancy and her

June-July 1989
A drama to teach the danger of free sex. Attempt to educate about AIDS.

friend Heidi were both in the drama—this in itself brought laughter and generally a lot of hoots! In the last act, the laughter came first. Tears came as the young star, Mike, died of AIDS after turning to the Savior. Of the over ten thousand students that saw the drama, about 250 came to know the Savior. A systematic program was organized to follow-up these decisions. It was a fantastic tool, and God used that script for the following three years. The principals at the schools reported that of all the efforts made by different organizations to teach students about AIDS, that particular drama brought more understanding and serious talk than any other.

****

In July we received a blessed surprise. Dick's brothers and sister collected enough money to pay for plane tickets so that Julie, Dick and I could come home during the month of August to celebrate his parent's fiftieth anniversary! We would be able to travel home with Nancy. Tim was also coming from Guatemala, so our family would be complete.

Dick has two of the most wonderfully godly parents in the world. Dad had been a farmer in North Dakota until 1952. He then moved his family to Santa Cruz, California. He owned a cold storage plant for five years. He picked apples and had once set the family record by eating thirty-two apples in one day! He worked in San Jose for a year reconditioning carburetors. In 1960 he and Charles Ottowa formed O&O Construction Company of Santa Cruz.

While in full support of her husband, Mom was busy with other things. She had been trained as a teacher and had taught in North Dakota. After marrying Everett, she was in for a shock! She had to cook for all of his brothers as they cared for large potato farms. But Mom had a heart of gold and soon was handling the job very well.

When the family moved to Santa Cruz, she had four children to care for. They wanted their children to grow up knowing the Lord. After attending the Methodist Church in town, they felt it did not preach the gospel and was very liberal. Where were they to go? Dick, their son, had been invited to "Sky Pilots." He enjoyed the club so much that he invited the whole family to attend church with him. The church was Twin Lakes Baptist. They felt right at home here and soon joined. Mom was very active.

Soon she was cooking for large affairs at the church and handling that very well also. Their home was always open to missionaries, friends, youth, and anyone that came along. Mom made home a refuge for many!

Dad and Mom both spent many hours upon their knees praying for their children. The love they demonstrated for each other showed their children how to love and gave them a very secure home. Their sincere love for God outshone all else. They both were active in the church and demonstrated signs of a humble servant's heart and effective leadership.

Dad and Mom first came to Uganda in 1971. They returned to Rwanda in 1981 where they lived for one year and helped build a power plant at the school. They had also done work in Central America and finally, in 1985, Dad had come to Uganda to help build Kampala Baptist Church. They not only served missionaries, but also became missionaries.

" . . . The prayer of a righteous man does prove effective and powerful" indeed. (James 5:16). Dick, their oldest son became a missionary; Linda is a teacher married to a professor at Moody Bible Institute; Paul, a pastor and a counselor in Ukiah, California; Joe, a physical therapist and a physician's assistant in the hospital in Ukiah. And Dad and Mom's love and prayers for their children have continued to this day.

In 1977, Dad and Mom Otto had moved from Santa Crus. Joe was a physical therapist in a hospital in Cloverdale, California. Mom had had some physical problems and wanted to be near to her doctor son. A few years later, Joe was transferred to Ukiah, California and so the folks followed. Paul decided to set up his counseling clinic in Ukiah and so the three families were all living in Ukiah at the time of the fiftieth-anniversary celebration.

At this celebration, Dad being seventy-eight and Mom seventy-one, we experienced dramas, food, memories, testimonies, and deep heartfelt appreciation for a couple that lived what they believed. The effect of their lives went far beyond what we could even imagine. We have a video of the parties and happenings of that day. I know the grandchildren were deeply impressed.

****

Dr. Goodgame concluded his work in Uganda that same August we were in America. Dick had agreed that the church Dr. Goodgame had held in his home could move to our place so the work could continue. By February of 1990 that group had grown so that our house was filled to overflowing—75 counting children! Since I felt my work at Kampala Baptist was not finished, I continued there. I would help set up the room at home for the worship service of Lugogo Baptist Church and then leave Dick to go to Kampala Baptist. I joined the congregation in our home for special feast and occasions.

In August of 1990, we experienced another momentous event. Julie was baptized! It happened at Kampala Baptist Church where there was a baptistery. Her dad did not do the baptism. He could have, but she thought it would be an honor to be baptized by her friend and pastor, John Ekudu. Julie had a radiant testimony of her love for her Lord and her desire to follow and obey Him.

Since Julie was home for her vacation, she helped us in a children's activity that we had during August. It was an overnight for the children at Kampala Baptist Church. We did *Psalty's Music Machine*, built the machine out of cardboard and old car parts, and presented the musical to the

153

church. Wow, did we have some wonderful times with the children and it was a special blessing to me to see how God was burdening the teachers—and Julie—for children.

The following month Julie wrote one of our prayer letters to the states. Let me quote her on a few of the items in it:

> Hi!
>
> How is life? Well, I am actually a junior, (don't worry, it's hard for me to believe I passed all those classes too). Soon to be Sweet 16 and never been . . . (Hey, at least my parents believe that). So, in one of my Dad's massive psychology books, it says I have my adult body now. I am hoping the book is lying, because 5'4" and 100 pounds? Come on, Lord, is this all I get? Oh, well, what can you do?
>
> Being away from home for nine months out of the year brings some times that are really great and some hard. Thanks for your prayers. I do want to be an encouragement to my friends and to grow in Christ. So keep praying!
> See you at the top,
> Julie Otto

****

Dick continued to disciple men. One of them, Barnabas Okeny, was growing and showing real signs of leadership. Nelson Okello also met with Dick and Barnabas and was an encouragement to them. Both of these men worked for the Uganda telephone company and were doing an excellent job there. Soon we could see that Barnabas was a great man of God, and he was called to be the pastor at Lugogo Baptist. In turn, Barnabas began to disciple men--Walter Odiro and Lawi.

Another ministry Dick could see growing was the care groups in Uganda. Dick feels strongly that people's needs are not met in a large church congregation. People need to be in small groups to really get to know and care for each other. Dick had been organizing groups of people both at Kampala Baptist and Lugogo to meet on a weekly basis in homes. In these meetings people shared what was happening in their lives, had a time of Bible study, and then a time of sincere prayer for one another. Members of these groups were soon sharing their deep needs and often helping one another with problems. There were over ten groups meeting in and around Kampala by Christmas of 1990.

It is a tremendous joy to be where God is working. Recently I have been learning that our prayer should not be "Lord, what is Your will for *my* life?" The question is "Lord, what is *Your will?* Where are YOU working?" Then we are to go there and allow God to do His work through us. (I might suggest a tremendous study for you. It is a book called, *Experiencing God* by Henry T. Blackaby and Claude V. King). I am convinced that that is where we were . . . in God's will. So many good things were happening, so many doors were opening, and there were so many blessings that we were overwhelmed.

****

I was trying to culminate my work at KBC and be sure that the teachers could carry on the work that had been established. I finally set a date in July of 1990 for a final concert performed by the friends I had worked with to say farewell. I then transferred to Lugogo Baptist Church to work more directly with the church there and with my husband.

1991 was full of examples of the wonderful things that happen when God is at work. Lugogo Baptist heard about a large home in Kololo that was up for sale for only $95,000. Most homes in this area cost from $200,000 to $500,000. The owner wanted the payment in three installments to be paid in March, October, and April the following year. The elders seriously prayed and we took the step of faith. We paid the first payment after receiving permission from CBInternational and the miracle of the money coming in! Then on March 24th, the church congregation moved in! Our home certainly could no longer hold the group that was 150 strong. Now we could prepare the room for worship on Saturday and decorate the entire building to look like a church. No longer would I have to rush around on Sunday morning trying to make my living room big enough for 150 people and appear churchlike.

In August 1991, Julie both saddened and delighted us. She was not coming to Uganda for the holiday. We would have to wait until December to have her home. She had been invited to visit Tim in San Francisco. His church was going to have a tutoring program for learning disabled children in the community. We were happy for Julie to have the opportunity to go to the states and be with her brother, but we would miss her.

We went to Nairobi to see Julie off and to begin a course of study with Azusa Pacific University. The course is called "Operation Impact." Azusa Pacific sends professors to over fifteen sites around the world to teach courses in the social sciences to missionaries and nationals. It involves "People Skills and Leadership Development." We had benefitted so much from our counseling in California that Dick decided to take the course. In three to five years by attending the lectures for two weeks a year and doing the rest of the work at home, a person could receive a master's degree. I was going along to just enjoy two weeks of rest but wanted to sit in a class to see what it was like. Oops! Wrong! You don't just sit in on a university course. You either take it for credit or audit—both cost money. So, I decided to take the class called "Conflict Resolutions."

This was God's will! He was in this and we were in "The Way." These courses were life challenging and benefitting—changing the course of our lives! We had first to attend for the five years it would take and then see what God had in mind.

****

I had been having the time of my life! In 1990 the youth choir at KBC wanted to do a musical called *Elijah*. So we invited the choir from Lugogo to join us. Then when I moved to Lugogo, I found a group of youth that were anxious to grow and *sing!* I love working with youth because it keeps me young.

Dick was still training men. In 1991 Greshon Olaboro joined the group. His wife had died and left him with a family of one son and six daughters. The church had stepped in to help at the time of his wife's burial and had shown real love to the family. Very soon Greshon sought out the church and the loving spirit that he had found in its people. One of our members led him to the Lord, and he wanted to grow in his belief. And grow he did! The man almost lived at our house soaking up Bible verses, talking, clearing up questions, and actually becoming one of our best friends. Dick and he went golfing together one day a week. We began to know his girls and see him change toward them. Usually fathers in Uganda have little or nothing to do with their children--other than the prestige associated with fathering many—but Greshon had changed. He was praying with them and trying to find out their needs. As I reflect on Greshon, I realize he had come to church with his family at Christmas 1989, so God had begun working in his heart even then. Jane, Greshon's oldest daughter was one of the active members in the youth group at Lugogo. I was enjoying getting to know her. She was shy but lots of fun and a very good friend.

****

A phenomenal answer to prayer came in September of 1991. One Sunday afternoon at 6:00, when some ladies from the church and I was returning from visiting one of our members who had just lost a sister, I stopped to let two ladies out of the car. The door to the driver's side of the van was yanked open and a man yelled at me to get out. At first, I thought it was one of the youth pulling a joke on me, but when I looked, I saw it was someone I did not know. I struggled a bit, refusing; he tried to force me, but then said, "Look!" When I turned toward where he had pointed, there was another man with a pistol pointed at my head only twelve inches away. Needless to say, all of us got out and watched as two thieves drove our Toyota van away. After the police reports were made, these ladies returned to their homes to pray. We found out that three families stayed up the entire night praying that our van would be found.

Monday morning, James, the business manager for our missionaries, drove into the yard yelling, "I saw your car! It is parked with the keys in it just down the road. The police are with it." God had miraculously answered our prayers and our car was returned to us. The gas was all used up, the spare tire stolen, and there was a large dent in the side fender. Later we learned the thieves had run into another car to stop it. They stole that car and abandoned our van. Praise to God for answered prayer.

****

Tim was actively involved in the Church of the Sojourners in San Francisco. Julie had had a wonderful time teaching children and getting to know her older brother much better. She was back at RVA to finish her last year. Nancy had graduated from Sacramento State and was working with the American Baptists. She was a counselor and coordinator for housing homeless people. She loved the work and felt she was learning double what the university had taught her!

The youth choirs at Kampala and Lugogo were preparing another musical, *Joseph.* And one of the young ladies there, Monica Kapiriri was writing an original musical, *Ruth.* People were growing and being trained.

Campus Crusade had made a film from the book of Luke called *The Jesus Film*, and we had shown it to the community around Lugogo Baptist. The church was actively involved in follow-up and counseling.

In Uganda, we were seeing more and more cases of AIDS and feeling the loss of many friends ourselves. Dorothy Nyeko, a precious saint and member of Lugogo Baptist, died leaving three girls ages fourteen, twelve, and nine. She was a nurse and had gotten the disease serving others. Her older sister had died just four weeks before. Francis, the young man that had been our Luganda teacher, had his father die in March.

Yet there were now over five hundred Baptist churches in Uganda! More care groups were developing. Leaders were being trained and taking over many responsibilities, thereby lessening ours.

By April 1992 the last installment for Lugogo Baptist Church had been paid! God had done the work. James 2:5 tells us, "Listen, my dear brothers: Has not God chosen those who are poor in the eyes of the world to be rich in faith . . . " My, how true this was. The elders at the church had prayed and miraculously the money had come in.

Julie would graduate in July and we would be bound for home. It had been a long four years, seven months, but it had been full of growth and joy. The only bad news about going home was that we couldn't speak up-to-date American English; we would get to hear only ourselves preach; most of the time we would live in a car, as a house; our personal devotional time would suffer due to lack of routine; and we'd miss our friends and co-workers in Uganda.

CHAPTER 18 – NEAR DEATH IN COLORADO

"Even though I walk through the valley of the shadow of death, I will fear no evil, for you are with me."
- Psalm 23:4

Dad Otto was eighty-one years young and Dick's life dream was to be fulfilled! Dick and his dad were going to build a home for us. A friend had drawn the plans and had them approved. We arrived in the U.S. in August 1992, after fulfilling a dream Julie had had—a week in Paris, France. This was her graduation gift. We stayed in the home of Bob and Mary Delamatta, CBInternational missionaries, and rode the train into Paris each day. As when we were in Italy, we enjoyed the tourist attractions of Paris—mostly on foot!

We arrived in Colorado in August to celebrate Mike's ninetieth birthday. Mike and Mom had been married thirty years, and the day after his birthday we celebrated their anniversary. Our three children, my two sisters, Martha and Laura, Laura's husband and my nieces and nephews were all there. What a glorious time of reunion!

August twelfth we arrived in Ukiah, California, just in time to enroll Julie in Mendocino Junior College, affectionately named Mendocino Tec! Dad and Dick immediately put up the guide strings for the foundation of the house. The next four months we saw the house raised and finished enough for us to move into in January. Dad outworked Dick, and I think was twice as excited about it all as well. What a man!

On weekends we had our regular routine of speaking at churches. I flew to Colorado to speak at the Rocky Mountain Women's Retreat there and to visit my stepdad and Mom. We got to San Francisco and Sacramento occasionally to see Tim and Nancy.

I think we had been away a bit too long. Nancy had experienced a great deal of depression and had struggled with that. I guess I will never know if our being there would have helped, but it was good to be with her now. She was slowly coming out of the depression and was doing a very good job in her business of cleaning houses and preparing them for new renters. She had not wanted to leave the work at the shelter because she felt she was really helping people, but it did not pay enough to live on. She started on her master's degree. But deep inside she was feeling a great loss. Read the feelings that she expressed and put on paper.

"Why??? . . . Where???"

I found myself, "well, in the depth of illness.

I found myself awake in the land of a gray hue.

I found myself laughing in the company of sorrow and tears.

I cried, "Don't make me leave this beautiful world where I can

touch that almighty and gentle one
. . . and go to the world of egos and
pride where there is no God!

Did I find it joyful because
I could be a Messiah?

Or did I find it joyful because I
could finally see my Messiah?

Was it the desire to stroke my
ego, helping the helpless,

or was it that the hopeless
taught me hope.

Lord, take me back to Your
people; the naked, hungry, poor
and prisoned so I can once again
worship You and learn Your hidden
knowledge."

By Nancy Otto, August 23, 1991

We were sent this poem long after the trauma she had experienced in changing jobs. It showed her desire to work with the poor. God was developing a great love for people in the heart of our daughter. But she would have to experience sorrow herself to really understand the poor and the trials they have.

****

Tim had found a real family within the church he was active in. He was one of the leaders and was training others. He also had a great part in the music and was learning to play the guitar very well. During the previous years he had attended University of San Francisco. At our arrival in the U.S. in August 1912, he had completed his nursing course and was a nurse at San Francisco General Hospital on the AIDS ward. Here he found the ministry was much more difficult but a great challenge.

****

We were greatly impressed with the care and encouragement shown by our churches. Everywhere we spoke we found genuine concern and prayer for the work we were doing in Uganda. Now we fully understood why our lives were so victorious and full. People were praying; God was fulfilling His will; and we were following His plan.

****

The following summer, July 1993, the Otto's had a family reunion in Minnesota. I do not mean the Everett Ottos—just twenty people. I am talking about 153 Ottos! We were looking forward to being in North Dakota and then Minnesota with all the crew. On the way Dick and I were going to stop in Yellowstone National Park to celebrate our thirtieth wedding anniversary. This is where we had gone for our honeymoon and knew it would bring back good memories. It certainly did! Old Faithful Inn was full to the brim with Japanese tourists--booked full even in March. So we took the Roosevelt Cabin and we almost died! It snowed while we were there on July 5th. A pass in the park was closed. The cabins had small wood burners, but we were allowed only two pressed logs a night! We just about froze to death!

****

One night at the reunion in Minnesota, Dick asked me to sit on the bed in our cabin. Julie and Nancy were there. Dick then knelt before me, took my hand and said, "Will you live with me for thirty more years of your life?"

Of course I will!" The tears were on their way. He handed me a small box containing a family ring—birthstones for the five of us. About then there was a real flood, and both Julie and Nancy clapped their hands furiously!

****

I am convinced that we were in God's will and that He was indeed using us to encourage our children, people in the churches, and our parents. We were heading back to California after a wonderful time of reunion with both the Otto's and my parents. Dick had gone into the mountains near

Rifle, Colorado, to have a day of fishing with his brother-in-law and sister. I was spending an extra day with Mike and Mom and then would join them at the cabin.

Many of the struggles we face are allowed by God to teach us needed lessons. Some things we fall into due to our own unrighteousness. And then I believe that occasionally Satan attacks. Satan is not pleased with God working in us, and he is actively trying to destroy us.

It was July 20th. We were to be back in California by the twenty-fourth so we could fly to Germany to take our Operation Impact courses from Azusa Pacific University. Taking the courses in Germany was about $5,000 less expensive than taking them at Azusa in California. I was looking forward to being near the Alps and enjoying fellowship with missionaries and nationals there.

As I drove into the mountains, it could not have been a more glorious day. There were pillory clouds in the dark blue sky, the mountains loomed majestically all around me, and the temperature was perfect. But I felt as if a strange dark cloud surrounded the car. In Dillon, Colorado I stopped the car and went into the shop to get something to eat. But again as I entered the car, I felt this oppression. I stopped and prayed.

"Lord, I do not know what is wrong, but I feel strange. I feel like there is something evil around me. I don't know why, because all along the road I have been singing and praising you for the beauty around me. I have a dark and eerie feeling. Please, I pray for protection and peace."

I continued the journey and soon was in Rifle. I had instructions on how to get to the cabin. I passed the fish hatchery and made my first turn. At the gate, I was greeted by a bunch of signs saying, "Do Not Enter!" "Private Property." "Anyone entering will be prosecuted."

Just then a car with two men and a woman came along. I asked them if there was a cabin on up the road.

"Yes, but it belongs to Mr. So-and-so."

"Do the Walkers live on past that?" I asked. "I had been told I would pass two cabins and then come to theirs."

"No, there is only one cabin up there and I wouldn't go if I were you. It seems that the signs mean what they say."

I spent the next two hours driving all around the vicinity, trying every road possible. Again, I felt that oppression. I stopped three times and asked God for protection and peace. I went back to the fish hatchery to ask directions from the ranger there. He could not understand the map but sent me to try one more road. No, that one was not it either. So back to the hatchery I went and called the Walker's home in Rifle. There was an answering machine.

"Hello. This is Ivy Otto. I'm lost! Actually I'm at the fish hatchery and will wait here for thirty minutes. I hope you show up. Otherwise I will come to your home in Rifle and wait there for you. Thanks."

I parked my car outside the hatchery on the road. While waiting I tried to pray and sing. I was discouraged but not really upset. I just could not understand the dark feeling I had. "Lord, I am counting on your protection and peace."

I had brought supper for all of us to eat at the cabin. It was in the back of the car. It was almost 6:00 P.M. now, and was sure Dick, Linda and Bill were wondering where I was. I waited the thirty minutes. I could not go back to the hatchery to call because as I left, the ranger had locked up and gone home. Well, I would go into Rifle and wait. I pulled out onto the road and everything went blank. Then as if dreaming, I opened my eyes to see a car coming straight at me.

Who was crying? I could hear babies crying. It seemed to be dark. I unfastened my seat belt to get out of the car and see what was wrong. The pain was excruciating! I blacked out. Again I heard the crying. This time I tried to open the car door, but it wouldn't open. I reached for the other door but passed out again. Finally, I heard voices.

"Don't worry, we will get you out of the car. Just relax."

My mind was a blank. What in the world was going on? I realized that if they asked me my name, I didn't know it. Slowly, over a period of about twenty minutes, it all began to come back to me. As the medics were calming me, cutting open the door, and trying to get me onto a stretcher being very careful to strap my neck onto a board, things began to fall into place. We were in America. We had built a house. Oh, yes, then we had traveled a lot—finally to North Dakota. My name? Ivy . . . Iva Jean . . . Ivy Otto! I had been with Mom. I had come up to Rifle to meet Dick. It was all back! By then I was strapped to the neck brace, on the stretcher, and loaded into an ambulance. My biggest worry was this. "They are really going to think I'm crazy. They will ask me what happened, and I don't know! Furthermore, when I tell them I've come to meet my husband, I will have to tell them I have no idea where he is!"

Evidently, when I pulled out onto the road, I passed out. High altitude? Stress? Sleepy? Absolutely not! I had been constantly praying and was relatively relaxed but certainly not sleepy. I wanted to find Dick and have supper! I believe Satan had been trying to kill me all day. But God had answered prayer—I had been protected, and I had perfect peace.

A son of the family owning the cabin had gotten the message on the answering machine. He had decided to come to my aid and direct me to the cabin. As he was coming, he heard on his radio about a terrible head-on collision. When he came upon the scene of the accident, he stopped. He asked if Mrs. Otto was involved. By then the medics and police had found my purse and my identity and told him I was not only involved in the accident but was in critical condition. He drove on to the cabin to tell Dick about the accident. When he talked to his dad, who was at the cabin, he reported, "She can't be alive!" Wisely, his father told him to tell Dick what the police had said. Dick was still fishing, so Linda, his sister, jumped in the car and came to the hospital. By the time Dick arrived, I was in the emergency room and conscious. I kept assuring them that I was okay and asking what had happened.

Apparently, when I passed out, I had crossed the centerline and hit an oncoming truck. Its occupants--a young couple with two children--were all okay. The wife had suffered a cracked elbow and broken jaw but was otherwise fine. The husband had one small cut and the children were totally uninjured. The wife had to be taken to the hospital for treatment, but the others had been released.

I suffered broken ribs, a partially collapsed lung, a severe cut across the neck, and one million bruises! They had to take me by helicopter to the hospital in Grand Junction, which was better equipped to treat me. I was in the hospital in Grand Junction for five days and then flown back to San Francisco. Needless to say I missed the trip to Germany. But I had Julie, and her friend Ruthie, from RVA to take care of me while Dick went to Germany. It was a long month in bed, but the girls provided excellent entertainment. Anyway, it was good for the girls. They would crack up every night as they had to put pillows around me, "just so" and then laugh as I held my sides to *keep* from laughing! Cruel!

Maybe it was Satan who had tried to kill me. I really do not know. We did hear that there is a lot of occult activity around Rifle. But God turned the accident into good. During the recovery, He became even more precious to me as I had lots of time to pray. I prayed for the young people that I had mothered. Little by little God showed me that I am to love them but not be dependent on them. I learned I could pray for these people and serve them but not become emotionally involved with them. The release was refreshing.

Julie had been accepted as a sophomore at Eastern College in St. David's Pennsylvania. She held a part-time job at Mendocino Hospital while attending school and had been able to save some money. When she arrived at Eastern, she received a grant from the school. CBInternational allowed us to give her $3,000 from our ministries account. With these and a gift from our church in Ukiah, the entire year was paid for! She would be able to save her hard-earned money for her junior year. Nancy and Tim seemed happy in their jobs and locations. Once again we were leaving the three kids in the hands of God for three years.

CHAPTER 19 – LOSSES IN UGANDA

"Precious in the sight of the Lord is the death of His saints."
- Psalm 116:15

"For I know the plans I have for you . . . "
- Jeremiah 29:11

When we got back to Uganda on September 20th, 1993, we found that the Lugogo church had gone to Gulu, two hundred miles north of Kampala, and planted a church! The church in Gulu already had a congregation of about one hundred people, and they were reaching out to two other areas to start churches. Lugogo itself was having Bible studies for both men and women and the church was growing—especially spiritually.

Our first safari was to Gulu to see the new church there. Dick began training five men from that area. Occasionally he would travel there; other times they would come to Kampala. Finally, he sponsored them to attend NIST (Nairobi International School of Theology) in Nairobi.

We also began having marriage enrichment seminars. Wow, those were really fun. Ugandans car hardly believe the Biblical view of marriage. It was so freeing to the women, and even the men to learn what God said their homes should be like.

Francis, our youthful language teacher, and Ruth, the daughter of a pastor in Kampala, were to be married in December. Francis had lost his father to AIDS. In December 1993, his mother had been killed in a terrible car accident while traveling to a funeral. Francis said her death was almost a blessing because she had begun to suffer from AIDS. The accident freed her from that suffering.

We were asked to be Francis' parents at his wedding. I got to make the cake for the reception. What fun! It was actually two four-tiered cakes connected with a bridge upon which bridesmaids stood. At the bottom was a church that I made at the request of the bride. I was proud of the cake. It served the 600+ people that attended the wedding. And Dick and I were happy to be the acting parents for this couple. December 7th, 1993 was the day and we all rejoiced. The week before we'd attended the wedding of another young couple, David and Trudi. I'd made their wedding cake too. The following week we were attending the wedding of David and Helen. What a fantastic privilege to see the youth we had worked with finding Christian partners. Now there would be more couples to counsel and guide in their new marriages.

****

I had been working with children during all my time in Uganda, but this term I designed a new children's program. It all came about as I prepared the papers for one of my classes in Operation Impact. It had been a burden on my heart for many years. Why weren't the Baptist churches reaching out to children? If they had any Sunday school at all, it was weak—and most didn't have one. Kampala Baptist had a good program. I had trained the people there. Lugogo Baptist had a good program, but I had also started that one. Agape Baptist, a sister church in Kampala, had a program because the pastor's wife had been at Kampala and been trained with those teachers.

For twenty-five years we had lectured about the need to have children's ministries. Yet, in the five hundred Baptist churches in Uganda, perhaps only five or six had viable programs. My idea was to start a children's choir of ten children. Two would come from each of the five Kampala churches. We would write a musical that addressed problems in Uganda. We hoped to travel to other churches to perform the musical. I believe that demonstration was a much better teacher than lecture. This was actually the research I did for an Operation Impact paper.

The story of our musical was about a young girl who had accepted Christ as her Lord and wanted to follow Him. However, her parents were not believers, and the father was an alcoholic. She faced much opposition in the family, but her friends were praying with her. Finally the father and mother saw love in her and decided to also give themselves to the Lord. We then showed the change in the family. Songs told much of the story. The children I chose for this group were very talented youngsters and did an excellent job with the music and the drama.

What fun we had! *The Baptist Kids Under Construction* were traveling and doing a great job. We presented the musical to about eight churches.

The news spread! We presented it to a pastors' conference in Masaka, and they went out challenging their churches to see what kids could do. We did run into a few problems. After our presentations I would ask the churches, "Do you have a children's choir?"

"Oh, Aunt Ivy, you know that our children aren't that bright. You had your special choir for a whole month to train them, and you are so talented! We could never do that!" was the frequent reply.

The next year I tried to solve that problem with *The Baptist Kids Stand Up*. This was a new group of kids. We would go to a church the day before the concert and include the children from that church. We taught them the songs in two hours, and they were a part of the program the next day! If the kids from these churches were smart enough to learn the songs in two hours, we were convinced that the teachers there could teach them as well!

To put "the icing on the cake," so to speak, we had a children's concert in January of 1996 and January of 1997. Each church presented a song from this children's choir. This meant that the teachers from these churches had to prepare a song on their own. Each choir also learned three of the same songs so that we had a mass choir. The first year we had seventy-four kids. The second year we had 127! Already people are asking about the concert in 1998!

****

Music in Africa is definitely different from that in the U.S. When we sing American music, the people enjoy it. When sing African songs, they are elated! Since I am also involved in leading music with the youth, I felt I needed to learn more about their type of music. That way I could encourage them to write songs that people would thoroughly enjoy.

I had the privilege of traveling with Dr. Roberta King from Daystar University in Nairobi. She is an ethnomusicologist. Her job is to learn the style of music that the people of a tribe or area use. She then challenges the songwriters, when writing Christian music, to use the same rhythm, style, and type of music the people love. This attracts the people to the music, but puts Christian meaning into action. It is an outstanding ministry.

We went to Soroti and Lira in Uganda. There we studied the finger piano (akongo) and the harp (adungu). We found entire bands in which only these unique instruments were used. We were thrilled with how well the nationals in the area learned to write their own Christian music. It was only a couple days time, but they were really communicating the gospel in a relevant way. Roberta is definitely an expert! ("Fundi" in Swahili!)

One man we met was blind. He played the akongo. It was unbelievable how good he was at it. He was so excited to hear that we were writing Christian music in their style. He picked up the songs almost immediately and the people loved it!

The youth at Lugogo Baptist knew how to play the adungu's. We were able to use the methods that Roberta taught and improve the music at Lugogo.

****

Significance. We felt that our lives were meeting needs and doing important things that have eternal value. June 19, 1994, our mission team was to meet at Lake Nabugabu for a conference and a day of fun. We would water ski, picnic, and plan for the next three months. Greshon, Dick's long-time friend at Lugogo Baptist Church, had been sick for about a week and on Friday was admitted to the hospital. We knew that his wife had died of AIDS, and he had infected her. Now he was also dying. We were driving out of the yard when his son, James, arrived to tell us his father was gone. He had been sick only ten short days.

Dick was broken hearted. This was his very best friend. Greshon had grown so much in the Lord and had become one of the leaders at Lugogo. He had six daughters age's twenty-two to six. James, his son, was twenty-four but was an alcoholic and certainly not interested in the welfare of these girls. But James was so shaken by his father's death that he began coming to church. He had seen the change in Greshon and decided that he really wanted the peace, understanding, and concern his dad had. In July he prayed to receive the Savior and began to grow much like Greshon had. As time went on we would see what God had planned for the Olaboro family. (Greshon is on the far left.)

****

In July a group from CBInternational called the Delta Team came to Uganda. The team consisted of six girls and one fellow. Julie had come back home after a good year at Eastern College. She visited friends in Kenya and then came to Uganda to work with the Delta Team. These youth had some wonderful experiences working with children and youth. After three weeks of intensive work, we took them to the game park in Uganda. As we were leaving we met a band of baboons. Foolishly, we fed them bananas. The largest of the pack jumped in the window of the van to get a larger share! I have never heard so many screams in my life! What is worse than a van full of seven girls, two fellows, and a baboon! Nothing! We threw the banana out the window and the baboon followed, but not until he had scratched the leg of one of the girls. They took pictures of her leg with signs pointing to the scratch! Probably this was their most memorable experience!

****

Dick was asked to attend Techny II in Illinois in August. It was leadership training for CBInternational leaders. There was no way I would miss out on a trip to the U.S. so we saved our shillings, and I got to go with him. Julie, Dick and I traveled back to the states together.

Again God had a plan in mind—or at least He knew what was coming. The fellowship there was uplifting. Dick learned a lot, and we got to spend time with Tim and Nancy again.

Nancy had purchased a home, but about the time we came, her business had collapsed. She was still attending Sacramento State University. Her desire was to get her master's degree in psychology and then her license in family and marriage counseling. We had begun to help her sell her home and get relocated, but it was time for us to return to Uganda. Nancy asked if we could stay just one more week to help her. We work for one of the most wonderful missions in the world! They granted an extended time to us, and our airline ticket was good for up to three more months.

When Nancy knew that we would be able to spend more time with her, she completely opened up to us. She was in a serious state of depression and had hit the bottom. She needed to be hospitalized but she had no insurance. The next best thing was for us to care for her and see that she recovered. We spent an additional six weeks and were able to leave Nancy in a much better frame of mind. God had known that we were needed here for a short time.

We made it through 1994 with many mysteries solved. Children's ministries were beginning to be important to the Ugandan leaders. Greshon's death brought James' salvation. A meeting in Wheaton brought us home at a time in which our daughter needed us. God does not made mistakes. It is such a privilege to be in His will.

****

My inappropriate mothering days had come to an end. God therefore led me into an appropriate mothering roll! James was so happy to have met the Lord that he realized he needed to help his six sisters. There were school fees to pay and food to be bought. James made a *lot* of changes in the days to come, but we saw immediately that James and the six girls would need guardians to help guide them through the struggles ahead. So now we were Uncle and Auntie to the beautiful Olaboro family.

James and Jane were Greshon's two oldest children, born to him by a village wife. James graduated from Nakawa College. He had a full-time job, although in Uganda even full-time jobs don't pay very much. Jane was the oldest sister in the family. She had a one-year-old daughter, Rita. We asked Jane to come and live in our servant's quarters and work for us in the evenings of the days Debra, our regular house-girl, was not here. The other girls were in school at various stages.

Greshon had taken a second wife, sometimes called the city wife, and by her had six girls. The fifth daughter died at age two. Julie, the firstborn, was attending school in Tororo, about one hundred fifty miles from Kampala. She was in senior five, which is the same as a senior in high school. Carolyn was in senior three at Gayaza high school, one of the best girls schools in Uganda. Stella was in Primary seven (seventh grade). Flora in Primary six (sixth grade), and Suzie in Primary one (first grade.) These five girls are brilliant! They were excellent students and were at the top of their classes. We soon found that the social skills of the two youngest needed a lot of direction.

By November James knew that the university would ask the family to leave the housing they had been living in. Since Greshon had been a university professor at Makerere University, the university had provided housing for the family. Now the children were homeless. Greshon must have known that he was HIV-positive because he had been building a duplex. In April he had rented out the side that was finished, so they had that small income from the rent. When the church realized the children's dilemma, they banded together and finished the other side of the house. Nelson and Barnabas, electricians who worked for Uganda Telephone Company, and elders at our church wired the house with electricity, and it was ready for them to move into.

During the year the girls would be in boarding school for a three-month term and home for one month. Things were settling in and were going okay for our new family.

One touchy thing happened to the family in June of 1995. Gloria, a former girlfriend of James', came to town. She decided to move in with James! Three days later when we found out, we went to James. He was struggling. He knew that as a Christian he should not have her there. Yet he did care about her. With a little talking, it was decided that Gloria would move in with Jane. After four weeks of Bible study, and much prayer on her behalf, Gloria too accepted the Lord as her Savior.

When school started again in September, Suzie, the youngest, was also in the house with Jane, Rita, and Gloria.

We had Suzie transferred to a new school. The aunties, who were sisters to the deceased mother, had been caring for Suzie but were no longer available to do so. So now, we had a new family—and a very cute, special little one, Rita.

Barnabas and Nelson were the key leaders at Lugogo. They both were men of integrity and worked for the telephone company. Barnabas had risen in responsibility at his place of work. He had been trained in many aspects of the company. But when a large foreign group came in to renovate the telephone system in eastern Uganda, they needed a trustworthy man to head the work there. Although Barnabas had been in electrical engineering, the company recognized his ability to work with people. They were also impressed by his integrity. They asked him to move to the East to become the manager of that new project.

We were happy for the promotion and trust Barnabas had acquired, but now Lugogo Baptist was without a pastor. Perhaps Nelson could step in, but he too was on the road so much that it would be difficult.

****

Our missionary team was growing. In 1993, Jan Huffaker, a single gal who had been in Indonesia for fifteen years, came to teach in our Bible school in western Uganda at Kiburara. She was doing a great job. We also knew that two new couples appointed to Uganda would be joining us soon.

In August 1995 Jan came through Kampala on her way to the Jinja Bible School. She was to teach there for a week. She had come early so she could have some physical tests done at the hospital here, because she was not feeling well. The doctor diagnosed giardia. Medicine was prescribed and in a day she felt much better. Then the sickness came back. This time the doctor thought perhaps it was malaria. Things were not very clear. She felt better and drove the fifty miles to Jinja. We received a call saying that she was sick again and would not be able to teach. She came back to Kampala and to the doctor. This time he had x-rays taken and found an obstruction in the bowel. But the doctor had grave concerns.

"Jan, you must go to Nairobi hospital there."

"But Doctor, I am so weak I can't possibly travel there.

"Your friend can go with you, and I will get a plane to take you out if you can't get a flight on Uganda or Kenya Air."

That evening Jan and I were on our way to Nairobi. I won't go into all the miracles that God did for us there, or the very long story of her illness. The sad thing was that treatment came too late. Any surgery would have killed her. She was full of cancer.

I stayed with Jan the two weeks it took her to heal sufficiently for her to travel and then saw her safely to the plane to return home to Arizona where she could be with family. Her brother-in-law, John Roper, came out to travel with her. On November 3rd, Jan was with her Lord.

****

In November we suffered another loss. Pastor John Ekudu was asked by the university to become the Dean of Students. John's appointment was the result of his integrity and proven leadership while working at the university. The school board had asked that he try to raise the moral standard of the school. It was a significant and great promotion for John, but now Kampala Baptist Church had no pastor. Dick was beginning to wonder why the best men--discipled and trained--were being taken by the government and other secular agencies.

****

Of the Olaboro family, Caroline was an outstanding example of what the love of Christ can do in a person's life. Everyone loved Caroline because she always wore a smile, never showed her moody side, and was there to help even before being asked. The teachers at Gayaza Girls School, where she was a student, were impressed by her hard work and loyalty to her classes and the many students. Other students continually sought her counsel and help in courses that were difficult. Her father had often remarked to us that Caroline was the most helpful in the home, and he felt she was one of the reasons he had desired to come to the Lord.

In October of 1995, Caroline came to our home very sick. We went to see her family doctor. He felt she was having heart problems and gave her medicine. She stayed with us one week, felt much better and was off to school again. The day after Caroline left, Jane wanted to speak to me alone.

"Aunt Ivy, I have just come from Family Doctor's Clinic. The doctor there told me that Caroline is HIV positive."

"Jane, it can't be!"

"You know the doctor at Family Doctor's Clinic is the school doctor. She was afraid of Caroline's condition, and so she tested her. Caroline does not know. Neither does our family doctor."

We were in shock. It couldn't be! Caroline was pure. We were certain of that! How had it happened?

Later when talking to the aunties, sisters to the girl's mother, they recalled a story. There had been a meningitis scare in Uganda. Some people had died. Mother Olaboro had taken the entire family to the clinic and gotten the recommended shots. When they reached Caroline, the needles were gone. So they used Mommy's needle for the injection. It was just a year later that Mommy died with AIDS. Now we knew how Caroline had been infected.

Caroline was sent home again. Some of the girls in S-4 (high school junior and Caroline's class) had misbehaved and so the entire class was to go home until the time of the exams. Caroline was with us for another week. By then she was having terrible tremors in the body. When the tremors came, she was terrified. I found that if I slept with her, I could hold her, and we would pray. During the calm times we talked.

"Auntie, do I have AIDS?"

"Caroline we are not sure. The school doctor thinks you do, but a more complete test must be taken before she is sure. Do you want to know?"

"I don't know. It means that I will not get better; I will die." And the tears came.

We talked about heaven and how both her mom and dad were there. If she did die, Jesus must think her job on earth for Him was finished. She would join her Savior, Mom and Dad. We read together. We prayed together. Slowly she began doing better emotionally. She studied during the day and taught herself to write with her left hand since her right hand was now paralyzed.

December third Caroline had her sixteenth birthday. I made her a cake to take back to school with her. I had noticed at church before we came home to pack, she had been crying. When I asked her what was wrong, she said, "I just want to be able to run again! But I know I never will! She returned to school for her S-4 exams. If she passed she would be allowed to go on to S-5 (senior in high school) and S-6 (First year of university.) Her final goal and dream was to pass the S-6 exams so she could be admitted to university. These were important exams. (In Uganda, you are admitted to the higher grades by passing exams. If you fail to do so, your schooling is finished)

Immediately after exams, she returned home. It was December 15th. All of the family was home now, but after a few days with them, Caroline wanted to come and stay with us. The home James lived in was small and Caroline was beginning to feel ill. By this time she was unable to speak complete sentences, was beginning to be paralyzed, and had to be helped with almost everything. We moved her to our guest bedroom where she had previously stayed. Her sisters came every day to help care for her and to prepare for the coming holidays. We made cookies. I can still see Caroline struggling with her left hand to decorate the cookies and tears come to my eyes. She was determined and still wore a smile

We had the family at our home for Christmas. Francis and Ruth also joined us, and it was a wonderful evening. We sang songs, put on our traditional Christmas play (Usually a comedy about Joseph and Mary, the camels, or some aspect of Christmas.) We had gifts, read about the beautiful birth of the Savior, and prayed together. Caroline sat on the couch and loved it all.

The next day the family went to church while I stayed with Caroline. Her sisters were growing weary caring for her, and she was beginning to have convulsions. Many times that day I held her tight and prayed. We stopped about twenty-five convulsions in that way. Now she could not talk at all and could no longer write. We had made special signs for certain needs and communicated that way. Oh, how precious she was!

After that day, we felt we could no longer care for her. We took her to the hospital. I will *never* do that again. The government hospital in Uganda is hopeless. We actually had to care for her ourselves in that desolate place. We stood by and watched Caroline suffer and finally enter the heavenly place where the suffering was over! We could only rejoice that Caroline was now running hand in hand with Dad and Mom as they showed her all around heaven. Jesus had greeted and hugged her closely. She now understood why she was home and she had no more regrets! We were all sad, but also glad to know that in heaven Caroline was rejoicing. Her suffering was over.

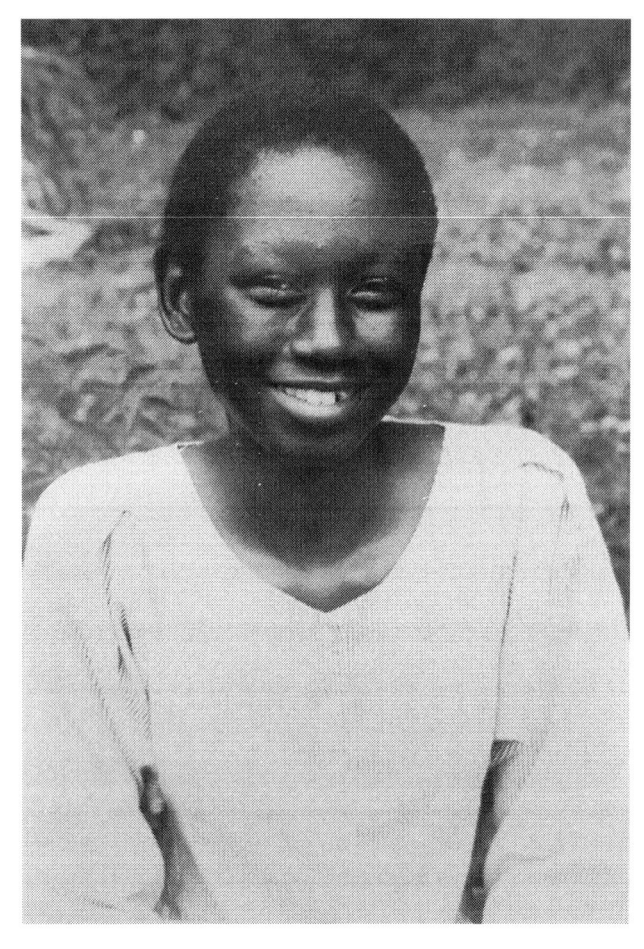

****

The years of this term in Uganda had taken its toll. We had lost to AIDS, a best friend and leader. We had lost two pastors to the government and better-paying jobs. We had lost a missionary colleague. And now we had lost one of the precious daughters God had just given us. But significant? We felt that knowing and working with these people had been terrifically significant. They were precious parts of the body of Christ. They were in God's will, had been used by Him, and would be used by Him. We had a fantastic feeling that our lives were significant.

1996 began with the funeral for Caroline. It is Uganda's custom to take to body to the village where the father was born. We transported Caroline's body to the village near Soroti, which is in eastern Uganda. It was the beginning of the binding of the Olaboro family closely together. The girls that went to the village ended up cooking for the people there as they grieved. Yet tradition says that people there should have been cooking for the girls who had lost their sister! The people there will long remember the testimony of these girls. They sang all the way to the village and back (about six hours one way)! To the amazement of all of us, Rita, who was now only two years old, began to sing these songs in the days to come.

January 12th we traveled with James and Gloria to her village. The groom must ask the father and family for the hand of the bride. Then a bride price must be agreed on. These people were rough! Having always lived in the western part of Uganda, they had never experienced war. Their homes were still intact and things were as they had always been.

James, on the other hand, was from the northeastern part of the country, and all they had ever known for the last thirty years was war. Their cattle had been taken, their homes burned, and life had driven many of them to alcohol. James, an orphan with no help from his village, was making his appeal to a man who had everything. The father had no way of understanding James' situation. He continued to tell how hard he had worked and explain that was why he had much. With little understanding of James' circumstance, he stood his ground on the bride price. He wanted $1,500 for his girl—four cows, six goats, and $500. He had given just a little because he began by asking for six cows, eight goats, and $700. We left the home happy that the agreement was settled, and James and Gloria could look forward to a wedding in about a year's time.

CHAPTER 20 – HOME ASSIGNMENT

"There is a time for everything, and a season for every activity under heaven."
- Ecclesiastes 3:1

February 1996 was time to go back to the states to visit our churches. We had begun the year with the funeral of our Ugandan daughter and the introduction (engagement) of our Ugandan son and his wife-to-be. The coming months were full of days of rejoicing and fun!

Our trip was a whirlwind! We arrived by plane in Philadelphia on Valentine's Day. Before we could even begin to get over the jet lag, Julie and Joe, a *very* special friend of hers, drove us to New York from St. David, Pennsylvania, to see a Broadway stage play. Having never seen a play on Broadway, even Dick was able to stay awake for it. But he slept both ways in the car.

We went from visits to their school, Eastern College, to dinner at Joe's, then off to stay with the parents of Julie's roommate for a party. Every once in awhile Julie would say, "Dad, has he asked you yet?" We were getting the feeling that Joe was about to ask us permission for the hand of our daughter in marriage! But it wasn't happening.

Finally on Sunday we visited Joe's church and met his parents. After church we went to a nice restaurant to get to know the parents better. It was February 18th, Joe's birthday. It didn't seem strange to us that the room was off by itself, or that the room was decorated with balloons. We were happy that the sister, brother-in-law and children all came as well.

Our visit was great. We heard the phenomenal testimonies of the parents, who had lived on the streets and in the drug culture, and how they had met the Savior. Eventually the table was cleared and we could see that some dessert was being put together. About that time, in walked a cow! Joe led the cow over to Dick and said, "Will this do?"

We had been writing to Julie and Joe. We knew that the young couple was seriously thinking of marriage. In Africa cows are the dowries for a bride. Yes, we had been teasing them that Julie was worth a lot of cows! We would never agree to less than her worth!

"She is worth a whole lot more than one cow, but I guess we will accept" answered Dick.

Joe then took the heart that hung around the neck of the cow, removed a small box from the center of the heart, and handed the box to Julie. I had been laughing and crying at the same time. When Julie opened the box, it was her time to scream and begin shedding tears just like her mother!

Immediately I knew that my son-in-law-to-be was creative! At that point, "the cow" asked if it could dismantle. Out of the costume stepped two of Joe's best friends. It was fun to meet them a bit ahead of the coming events. Andy was Joe's roommate, and RB is a youth pastor. Joe and RB had been in many classes together since both are taking the youth ministries course at Eastern University. Joe is a youth pastor at his church in Vineland, New Jersey.

We had to continue our travels the next day. But we would be coming back to visit Julie and Joe a few more times before our return to Uganda. We went to Wheaton to meet with the doctor — medical doctors as well as Ph.D.'s in the mission. All of our meetings were pleasant and a great encouragement to us. I've said it before, and I'll say it again, CBInternational is a great mission. The directors truly try to understand and work with each individual missionary but have a vision that can stretch us all. They know how to listen and to guide. They are interested in the work we are doing but challenge us to greater things. Our time went very well.

****

My stepdad, Mike, was growing weaker. But at ninety-three and a half years, who wouldn't be? He still could tell delightful stories of when he was young and growing up on the farm, funny stories of his first long ride in an automobile, contrasts that he has seen in his lifetime. He was also talking about heaven a great deal these days and was anxious to go there. We stood and wondered how much longer this godly man would be with us. Each night we still read the scriptures and a devotional out of *Daily Bread*. More often than not, it was Mike who read.

Mom, at eighty-three, was doing much better, still sewing together quilt blocks that the women in the community center cut for her. In about a week, she would have another quilt top ready—all beautifully matched designs. Off it would go to the center to be quilted and tied. Each week she also made an afghan and a child's sweater! She claims it is easy to do. She does it while she watches the Denver Rockies baseball team play their games. She cared for Mike daily and seemed happy in their home. It was getting harder for her to get out because Mike would so often fall, and she needed to be there for him.

As Dick and I visited these two precious parents in Colorado, we wondered how we could be of more help to them. We also worried that Mom would not be able to take care of Mike much longer. Dick and Mom sat and talked about some options. Mom loves Dick. It seemed that she was happy to have two sons-in-law! In her eyes, I'm not sure Dick or Micheal, my sister Laura's husband, could do any wrong.

But we had to move on after only four short days. We promised them that we would be back in May, right after Julie's graduation. We would be with them a week as we had to speak at two of our churches in the area.

Nancy met us in San Francisco. It had been her birthday the day before—February 28th—so Tim and Talitha, her cousin, had driven up to San Francisco to join the party. Finally, after two and one-half years we were with our two older kids again. It was wonderful to see them. And guess what? God, as usual, was way ahead in meeting our needs. Tim had driven up from Sacramento a re-conditioned car that Bruce Clatterbuck, our Northern California Director, had worked over! We now had our car for the coming six months.

We drove on up to Ukiah the following Monday to finally be in our home for the six months of furlough. Whoops, I mean "Home Assignment." It was more than relaxing to be back with Dad and Mom Otto, but we knew there would be lots of building, excitement, jobs, talking, and meetings ahead. You just can't hold those two parents down!

****

"What can I do?" I asked the doctor?

"You will just have to live with it. The arthritis is there and there isn't much you can do. I will give you these muscle relaxants."

"But, Doctor, some people say that I could have a hip replacement.

"Out of the question! You should wait fifteen years before you do that! Just learn to live with the pain."

That was in early 1994. I had had intermittent pain in my right hip. Sometimes it would "catch," and I would almost land on the floor! I wasn't a complainer, but it did make my work more difficult. The doctor had told me to wait, so I had gone back to Uganda with the problem. I did stop playing volleyball and taking long walks. But I kept up with my tennis games!

Now, two and a half years later, I knew something was indeed wrong, and I went back for a checkup.

"Boy, the doctor is really going to say something interesting when he sees this X-ray! He told me there is really nothing wrong with you. You just have a hard time with a little pain." This was the comment of the X-ray technician. But I had been to the doctor before, and he seemed to show little concern and gave few instructions, so I didn't expect he'd say anything interesting when he saw the X-ray.

"Well, let's look at these X-rays together," said the doctor. "Oh, my!" As his mouth dropped open!

Bone on bone. The only remedy was—major surgery, which took place on April 1st. Not a very choice day because, believe me, it was no joke! Since then I have a greater understanding of *major – really MAJOR pain!*

I was unable to attend church on Easter Sunday, and the next Sunday Dick went to Pioneer, California, without me, much to my displeasure. But by the third weekend, I was on crutches and went to a seminar in San

Francisco—traveled on to Tracy, California, for a mother/daughter banquet. God is good!

We love visiting our churches and sharing all the great things God is working on in Uganda. I love being with kids and youth—challenging them to walk with the Lord into great adventures! Urging them to God's will, to obey Him so they can get in on real action. I had a super time at that banquet. I will admit that I sat a lot.

****

During the whirlwind of speaking every Sunday in one of our supporting churches, we did take the time to travel to St. David's, Pennsylvania, to attend Julie's graduation. Thus began a series of exciting events. One was that we stayed with Lisa Nesspor's parents. Lisa was one of Julie's roommates at Eastern. Her parents lived about thirty minutes from the school. They welcomed us into their home again this second time.

As we visited, they expressed their willingness to open their home for Julie's wedding. Of course they were in on some of the discussions concerning the wedding. Julie wanted to have it on Eastern's campus. It is extremely beautiful—lakes, fountains, green hills of grass, and streams. But the gazebo that had been a part of Joe and Julie's courtship, had been taken down. The cost of using facilities at the school would be reasonable, but more than we felt we could pay. Then terror of terrors—we heard all the roads throughout the campus were going to be repaired come summer! So that just about did it. We would at last consider having the wedding in the backyard of the Nesspor's.

****

Julie and Joe figured out that if Joe didn't travel with us to Colorado and California after her May 4th graduation, he really wouldn't get to know the rest of the family or us. I had planned to spend about three weeks with Julie at Nesspor's just before the wedding. Dick would be there only one week before, and of course after the wedding, Joe and Julie would be off on their honeymoon. We knew that would be the last time we'd see them before returning to Uganda. So, it was all arranged—Joe would go with us to our churches in Colorado and then on to California.

The excitement was running high for me. I would get to introduce our son-in-law-to-be to my mother and stepdad. I knew they would not be able to come to the wedding, so I was ecstatic! But can you imagine the thrill for Joe? Here was a kid that had grown up on the streets, and then after the Lord called him, had been only on the East Coast. He had never traveled. He had been in a plane only one time. He had heard about the beautiful mountains of Colorado, but never dreamed he would see them. Later Julie shared with us that he sat glued to the airplane window! This greatly amused Julie since she had spent much of her life on planes. This kid who'd grown up amidst third-world cultures would have so much to learn from the stateside kid she was about to marry. But he would have much to learn from her too.

I had not forgotten the beauties of the Rockies, and I will never tire of them. Their magnificence can only have come from our God and creator. I stand amazed every time I gaze upon them. We took Joe and Julie to see the Red Rocks and then on to Camp Id-Ra-Ha-Je. We walked around camp—went to see if the PowWow Chapel, overlooking the valley, was still in existence at Teepee Camp. It was! Now it was made of cement so it would last longer.

We spent the late afternoon and night on Hamilton's ranch. When I was teaching Bible school in the Colorado mountain towns, I had lived with the Hamiltons near Fairplay. They had become life long friends. I don't think there are many people in the world that have ridden a cow! I don't mean a cow like the one Joe gave us—I mean a real one! The niece of Doug Hamilton, who had been the ring bearer in our wedding, had a trained cow. It had been an orphaned calf and the children had played with it. It was taught to pull wagons, kneel, shake hands, and gallop. Now, although it was a mommy cow and had its own little calf, it was still up to its tricks! Joe and Julie took a ride. It was also fun to share our new son-in-law-to-be with this very special family.

The next day we drove over Kenosha Pass, past Breckenridge Ski Resort, up over the old Loveland Pass that Dick had backed down to start the rental truck! We then drove up to Echo Lake and over Squaw Pass. In May much of the snow was still on the passes. We took pictures in the snow — twelve feet above our heads — and soaked in all the mighty work of God.

Joe got to go to church with us and hear our spiel, as Julie calls it. Although she teases us a lot — mainly because we share much the same talks in each church — she enjoys it.

On to California, Joe escaped being locked up at Alcatraz, but enjoyed the visit. In San Francisco he got the thrill of his life! One day while walking in town with Tim and Julie, they entered a guitar shop. After looking around a bit, Tim informed him that he was to pick out one. This was going to be his wedding gift. Joe couldn't believe it.

Dad and Mom Otto highly approved of Joe. The nieces and nephews were enthralled with his professional drumming, so I guessed he was "in." We also knew that Mom Otto would not be up to traveling to Pennsylvania, so it was special that Joe could be in California, and they could get to know each other. Then it was on to Sacramento for a special graduation party for Julie put on by Nancy. Joe was thoroughly initiated into the family!

****

Please don't become annoyed with my frequent repetition of this statement, "God is so good" because He is! Julie was going to be in California for just five weeks. There is no way that you can get a job for just three weeks — unless God does it. And He did! The first week we stayed in Sacramento to purchase things we needed for the wedding. Then we returned to Ukiah. Julie stopped in at the hospital where she had worked while going to Mendocino College. Would she work, they asked. Would she! The people she knew there were happy that she would be able to help out even for three weeks. She knew the job — they knew her. So, Julie got back her old job at the same good wage and put a few dollars into the kitty for her wedding.

It was back to St. David's in June. By now I was on only one crutch and able to do a few more things. We had a great time being with Sue Nesspor and her fun-loving husband, Tom. Sue and I were becoming great friends. We stayed at their place long enough to set them at ease about the details of the wedding and finish the arrangements there. Then Julie and I were off to Vineland, New Jersey.

****

    I won't tell you all the miracles of the house in Vineland. I will just say that out of twenty-two rental applicants—one of them being a relative of the owner—Joe and Julie got the house! They actually had been refused, but due to the failure of Joe receiving that message, Joe went to meet the owner and after meeting them in person, he changed his mind. During the next week and a half, Joe, Julie and I had much fun putting the place in order. As gifts, they received couches, chairs, tables, and beds. They weren't all of their choice, but with a little creativity and a trip to the Salvation Army, the decorating of the house turned out rather nice. The most fun was making the kitchen cabinet that doubled the storage space for the wonderful gifts they had received at four different showers. God has supplied my needs for years. Yet, I think a greater thrill is to see God provide for my children—apart from me!

****

    The wedding was of course the most beautiful wedding in the whole world. We teased Julie that she had more people in the wedding party than in the audience, which was almost true! She had asked nine girls to be her bridesmaids—her sister, Joe's sister, three girls from RVA days, her two roommates from Eastern and two other friends. In the end, Joy from RVA couldn't attend. Joy was off to Estonia with the Peace Corps and had to leave two weeks before the wedding.

In each aspect of the wedding, God provided. After looking at forty-three dresses, all which had to be altered and cost over $500. Each, we found one she could order! It was $350. The quote of over $3,000 for photos was taken care of by my brother-n-law and Tim so it cost us only the price of the film. We got over twelve hundred pictures, plus forty-four 8 X 10's for about $300 instead of the thirty-five pictures for $300. Okay, okay, I can say we had a $10,000 wedding for about $2,000.

Nespors' backyard could not have been groomed more beautifully. A friend in Christ had brought in a gazebo. The church supplied the kitchen in which to prepare the food and the chairs and tables for the feast. People said it was one of the most delightful weddings they had attended. It was beautiful but relaxed.

The only real hitch in the wedding was the birdseed. Since throwing rice is a no-no these days, a friend had gotten birdseed. However, she had failed to read the label correctly. It said, Treated bird seed, for getting rid of birds." When hot peppers got in Julie's eyes and Joe's throat, they ran for the water to rinse it out!

    I will admit that we cried at the airport when we watched them go off for their honeymoon in Florida. Julie started it! She cried and waved at us all the way up the escalator as we stood below crying and waving. Poor Joe. He was trying his best to comfort her but to little avail. Parting is never easy. It would be another three years before we would see them again.

****

    We had one last trip to make. Drive the car from California to Chicago for meetings, and to where Joe and Julie would pick it up. It was our gift to them. We would not get to see them because we had to fly on Thursday. Joe and Julie would not arrive to pick the car up until Saturday. Our plans were set—then came the call.

    Mike was in the hospital. It looked as if this would be the end of his time on earth. My sisters really wanted us to be there. So, we left California a week early. Dick would have to fly back for four meetings, but at least I could be with Mom and my sisters. We left early Monday morning, had a flat near Salt Lake and found out we needed two new tires. Unexpected purchase, but we bought them. Monday late afternoon we had another blowout! Yep, in Wendover, Nevada we had to buy two more tires!

    We got into Golden, Colorado at 9:00 Tuesday evening. Mike had gone home to be with his Savior at around 10:00 that morning. It was a blessing. At ninety-four years old, he had grown tired and wanted to be with the Savior. He hated leaving Mom, but it was best.

    Laura, my sister, had been with Mom for almost a week. Micheal, her husband, and Marti were coming on Wednesday. We helped with many of the arrangements. Mom was doing very well. Dick had to fly back to California on Thursday so he missed the funeral on Friday. But it was a good time of being together as a family and we praised God that we were with Mom and not in Africa.

CHAPTER 21 – GOD'S REWARDS

". . . then I am strong."
-2 Corinthians 12:10

God is good! When Moses and the Israelites crossed the Red Sea, God was credited with the marvelous miracle and received all the glory, but the Israelites got to take the dry hike! When Daniel was thrown to the lions, again God was praised for the astonishing miracle and was given the glory worthy His name, but Daniel got to pet the lions. God certainly is responsible for all the miracles in my life, and is more than praiseworthy of the glory due His name, but I got to be there!

In all of us there is that part that realized the worthiness of God; the miraculous honor due His name; His holiness, righteousness, and justice; His sovereignty; and on the other side, we have the privilege of being His child and seeing in our own lives how He is at work in us to make us like His Son. God has allowed me to see a few of the fruits that have come as a result of my walk with Him. I'd like to share just a few so that again you too can rejoice at the wonder of God.

****

In July I received a letter from Kilani, the Hawaiian fellow that had organized the Lei O'Lima teams to go to Maui in 1957 and 1958, who wrote to me. In his letter he included a second letter from Helen France. Helen had been with us on Lei O'Limas I and II. She and her husband serve with Wycliffe Bible Translators.

"Dear Kilani,

I wanted to send an extra note to you since I have a very special story to tell you . . . At our Wycliffe missions meeting I met a member, Fran Wakefield. Since we had not met before, I asked her some basic questions. When she told me, 'I was born in Maui, Hawaii.' my ears pricked up as you can imagine. Then I mentioned that I had been to Maui on a Gospel Team in 1957. Before I could get any further, she said, 'Oh, you were with the Lei O'Limas!' That began the most wonderful and fun time of talking as we connected from so many years ago.

"Fran said she remembers those who came to her church. (She was in 8th grade at the time and remembers the 2nd team the best). She could name off the people in the quartet and trios and that girl who played the trumpet!"

I was in the singing groups as well as being 'that girl who played the trumpet!' This young lady said she felt the Lei O'Limas and other Gospel teams were what helped her in her spiritual walk.

****

While we were in Oroville, we saw a young mother come to the Savior. We began teaching her and praying for her husband. The closest we got to the husband was to play together with him on our church softball team. I received a letter from Arlene when we were in Uganda.

"Dear Dick and Ivy,

Hi! I know this letter should have been sent years ago. . . .

I just realized I didn't even mention Rick! (her husband). Oh, Ivy, I never dreamed Rick would ever be a spiritual man. When you pulled him in with your baseball tactics, you had a man with a lot of hurt, vengeance and no love. Today he is a caring, giving man with extreme wisdom. And yes, he's still that boy at heart but he's a man now.

Our deepest and sincerest love and gratitude.

Rick and Arlene.

Last Sunday a young man sat in my living room and shared the following story. He had just been admitted to Makerere University as an adult student. He had applied along with three thousand other people. Only five hundred were to be chosen. He had been one of the five hundred. He is taking the music course.

He said, "Thank you, Aunt Ivy! When I auditioned for piano, I was asked, 'Who taught you?' I had to say, Aunt Ivy. When I played my trumpet they were really surprised. 'Where did you learn to play like that?'

Again I had to tell them that Aunt Ivy had been my teacher. I really don't know how to thank you enough.

Paul had been in my Sunday school class and participated in most of the musicals we produced. Now thirteen years later Paul is teaching music to students at Kyambogo College and had been accepted to work towards his B.A. at the university.

Many of the women in my Bible study classes had never been in small groups like this before. Because of the sharing of problems and prayer requests, they grew very close. They said before, they had gone to neighbors to help with their problems but it had never really helped. But in this group, people gave good solutions because they turned to God. They had never before experienced such help and love.

Of course as a mother, I think the biggest blessings are the fruits I see in my own children . . . my biological kids and those others God has given me along the way.

Tim, our firstborn, with bright red hair and freckles, plus his sweet, obedient attitude, was greatly appreciated by his parents. Tim received all "A's" only because of his diligence. He loved giving speeches and has many trophies to prove his ability. As student body president at Oroville High school, he developed great leadership skills. His love for the Lord and witness at school definitely helped to build the new church Dick was seeking to plant. Upon his graduation from High school, we were going back to Uganda so Tim was left here in the states to attend University.

At Biola University he aimed to be a lawyer and politician, but found it was not his gift. After graduation he went on some mission trips, which sparked his interest in ministry. Today he is an active member and leader of an inner-city church in San Francisco. While in San Francisco, he trained as a nurse and also serves at San Francisco General Hospital. I can't begin to record the wonderful heartfelt letters he has sent us through the years.

Nancy, our second born, surprises us and makes us thankful that we also had a red-haired daughter. She has always been the lively, social one. Her grades in school were all acceptable, but she certainly spent most of her time making and being a friend. Perhaps that's why today she is a social worker!

Nancy was always active in the musicals we put on at the churches we served in. She loved to sing and did sing many solos. After being in Oroville, she got to go to Uganda with us and entered as a sophomore at Rift Valley Academy.

Those years at RVA developed many lifelong friends. She was active in basketball, volleyball, and field hockey. Upon returning to the states, she attended Biola for a year and a half. Due to the cost of tuition and room and board, Nancy then transferred to Sacramento State.

Nancy has struggled with many issues—romance, changing schools, changing majors, and depression. Realizing she had a great love for the poor and the social work she wanted to do, it became a bit much. Yet, with further investigation, she found that the basis of her depression was more physical than emotional. In experiencing some really down times—the loss of her business—Nancy fully understands the struggles that the people she works with have to face. God, in His gracious love, allowed Nancy to go through some dark valleys to be able to better understand the people He has called her to work with.

Nancy is actively involved in Fremont Presbyterian Church in Sacramento. She also has Bible study groups in her home. One surprise for me was in a letter she wrote: "Mom, this is a treble clef. (Hee hee!)" She is finally taking piano lessons! I tried for five years to teach her to no avail! But, oh, what great joy in having such a priceless daughter.

Julie. Too many people, just to speak her name bring delight. She is the one who served tea to guests when the folks weren't home. That little girl, who, by the way, is now twenty-two—no, not fifteen—is the wife of a youth pastor, working as a waitress but looking for a job in social work. God, how can one couple, we, be so blessed?

****

I could talk about the exciting wedding that is coming up in January—James and Gloria. Or about how excited Jane is when she comes home every day, telling what she has learned at YMCA. I could tell you how proud I am of Julie Olaboro, who is at Makerere University. Only about two percent of the youth that pass their exams make it to the university!

Or I could tell you about Stella—that precious girl that desires more than anything else to live like Christ.

Or Flora, who is number two in her class and asked, "Auntie, how do you share Christ with girls that are not so interested . . . you know like Catholics? She goes to a Catholic school and was shocked to find that some students there aren't interested in spiritual things.

Then there is Suzie—oh, precious little Suzie. So many heartaches in life before she turned nine . . . Mommy died when Suzie was only two; Dad spoiled her because he was hanging on to the lastborn of the wife he loved. Then he died when she was only six. At age eight, her loving sister also died. Is life worth living? Oh, yes! And we can see it in her eyes as the days go by.

Rita. Well, Rita is the only grandchild. You know how people can go on for hours about a grandchild? Do you know she sings perfectly in tune all the songs we sing at church? And do you know that . . . ?

God is good. There have been many miracles He has performed--many millions of answers to prayer. He is to be praised. But praise Him too that He has allowed me to walk along with Him and bear fruit . . . much fruit!

CHAPTER 22 – PRAISE

"Let everything that has breath praise the Lord.
Praise the Lord."
- Psalm 150:6

My first PRAISE TO GOD is for *asking me to write the story of my life.* And that He timed when it should be written. Way back in 1982 I was doing a study in 2 Corinthians. When I came to verses nine and ten of chapter twelve, I was amazed at the contents. It seemed to me that my life fell perfectly into the words used there to express what Paul delighted in . . . weaknesses, insults, hardships, persecutions, and difficulties. And while I reflected on this, I remembered that essay I mentioned in the forward, the one I had written in my senior year of high school, "What I Expect to Accomplish by the Time I'm Fifty." Then I realized that I was almost at the golden age of fifty. Why not write what had actually happened?

I began back then to write with the goal of completing it in 1988, in time for my fiftieth birthday. Many things entered my life since then: laziness, fear of writing, learning to use the computer, and then the war that made us hide all computers, loss of interest, lack of time. But I was challenged to complete it for a college course. In that circumstance I knew I would do it, for I always do best under pressure or when given an assignment.

God had His plot. He gave me experiences to complete the verse, "For when I am weak, then I am strong." 2 Corinthians 12:10b. In fact, as you have seen, the "For when I am weak," chapter 15, was the longest and perhaps the most maturing time in my life. Thank you, Lord; I PRAISE YOU!

I PRAISE GOD *for all I have learned about my own life.* This is not a bird's-eye view, but a mustard seed's view. My life has been so full that when I began looking in the *very few* scrapbooks and memory books that are here in Uganda, I realized that I didn't even *begin* to cover my life. And then, horror of horrors! I have about thirty more scrapbooks, picture albums, and memory books in America! I have learned that my life has been more than full! I have learned that if I were a facile writer, I could write hundreds of books. I feel like John: "Jesus did many other miraculous signs in the presence of His disciples, which are not recorded in this book. But these are written that you may believe that Jesus is the Christ, the Son of God, and that by believing you may have life in His name." John 20:30-31. I guess I could write, Ivy 20:30-31 "God gave Ivy one million other blessings and experiences, which are not recorded in this book. But these are written that you may see a few of the things God wants to teach all of us by the time we are fifty."

As I wrote, God continually encouraged me. At one point I thought I should stop, but that day God gave me these words from *Psalms/Now* by Leslie F. Brandt, Published by Concordia Publishing House, St. Louis, 1986. (All of the Psalms quoted in the remainder of this chapter are from *Psalms/Now*.)

Psalm 110 "God spoke to me today. He broke through my childish doubts with words of comfort and assurance. 'Hang in there; sit tight; stick to My course for your life, 'He said, "I will not let you down." He reminded me of how He cared for past saints, how He watched over them and kept them through their hours of suffering and uncertainty. He reviewed for me my own life, His loving concern through the days of my youth. He restated for me my commission and appointment. His trust in me as His servant in this sorry world. He reiterated His gracious promises to stand by me, to empower and support me in the conflicts that await me. I know that God is with me today—just as surely as He was with His saints of old. I have neither to fear nor to doubt the eternal love and presence of my Lord."

So with God's encouragement and strength, I hung in!

****

What exactly is it that God needs to accomplish in each of our lives before a destination like Uganda can be obtained? Salvation, obedience, to begin making us like Christ, teaching us we must choose, trust, and rest. I think that I can summarize it using examples in my life.

I PRAISE GOD *for my salvation and what that involved.* John 15:16 says He chose me! I could see He had because of the deep desire I had to know about God even before I knew Him. I could see it in the experiences God gave me with my parents and family.

Matthew 28:18-20 gave direction to Pastor Bob Peterson and Uncle Paul, which they obeyed. Therefore I was found by the Lord and accepted His gift—the call to become His disciple. I received salvation. I just asked forgiveness for all the sin that was weighing me down and turned from it to follow Jesus. It involved obedience. I was baptized and began to learn His commands. The commission to go and make disciples, baptize them, and teach the commands was then passed on to me. "And the things you have heard me say in the presence of many witnesses entrust to reliable men who will also be qualified to teach others," 2 Timothy 2:2. And I obeyed the command. This was a joyous privilege! He had created me, loved me, and called me to Himself. His love for me was so strong that it actually compelled me to carry it to others.

I PRAISE GOD *for His command that I am to love the Lord my God.* "Jesus replied: "Love the Lord your God with all your heart and with all your soul and with all your mind. This is the first and greatest commandment." Matthew 22:37-38. God wants a deep relationship with us! I am so thankful that as a youth I chose as a life verse Philippians 3:10 "That I may know Him . . . " Since this was the ultimate goal for my life, I was obeying the command to love Him with all of me!

God's maximum desire for mankind is that we love Him. You see, we often think that man is god-less. That is true, and it is the reason why we need salvation. But actually, God is man-less! God wants us! God loves us! God wants a deep relationship with us! That was the "why" of the cross. "I have loved you with an everlasting love; I have drawn you with loving kindness!" Jeremiah 31:3. Leslie Brandt has put words to my response:

Psalm 18 "It is no wonder that I love you, O God. You have granted me a security that I could never find among the things of this world. You have erased from my life the fear of death. What follows the grave is not my fearful concern. The traumatic experiences of this life cannot destroy me. You are never out of reach but are ever aware of my problems and conflicts. How great and all-powerful is my God!

> . . . I rejoice in His concern and love for me. I will proclaim, O Lord, Your praises to anyone who will listen to me. I will sing and shout and dance in the joy of knowing that You are my God."

In my relationship with God, He taught me to pray. He taught me to read and deeply study His Word. Uncle Paul was responsible for fostering my deep desire to know the Word. He taught me to memorize scripture; he challenged me with his roleplay as an unbeliever to answer all his questions with scripture; I was always in Bible drills where the contest was to see who could find the passage of scripture fastest. Yes, I soon began to realize that in His Word were all the principles I would need for life.

As I experienced His closeness and knew He was walking with me, my trust in Him grew. He was with me through all of 2 Corinthians 12:10 . . . weaknesses, insults, hardships, persecutions, difficulties. Weaknesses make us strong.

" . . . Love your neighbor as yourself" Matthew 22:39. Definitely God's second great command is that He wants us to love this world as He does. We need to see the world through His eyes.

> Psalm 119 "I can truly love You only inasmuch as I proceed to love Your children in this world. I can serve You only as I commit my life to service on behalf of my brothers and sisters. I can offer sacrifices to you only by way of the altar of my neighbor's need. This is Your law, Your standard, Your design and will for my life.

Very early in life He taught me that people are to love; things are to use. And He kept taking things away from me and giving me people so that I would learn it! Never are we to love things and use people. Thank you Lord for teaching me that!

I am thankful to God that He helped me to see the world as He sees it by sending me to Hawaii and then to Africa! And, oh, the delight and joy I have found in the people He has brought into my life and continues to bring. They are priceless, encouraging, and beautiful!

Finally, I PRAISE GOD that He is *making me like Christ*. Never read Romans 8:28 without verse 29. It does not make sense without verse 29.

"And we know that in all things God works for the good of those who love Him, who have been called according to His purpose. For those God foreknew He also predestined *to be conformed to the likeness of His Son. . ."* In fact, I think it hurts many people when verse twenty-eight is quoted alone. *Everything* does work for the good to those of us who have been called according to His purpose, but *only* because by all these *things* we are being conformed to the likeness of His Son! God wants us to be complete—as is His Son. He is in the business of making us like Jesus.

We are commanded to have the same attitude as that of Christ Jesus: "Who, being in very nature God, did not consider equality with God something to be grasped, but made Himself nothing, taking the very nature of a servant, . . . He humbled Himself and became obedient to death—even death on a cross! Philippians 2:6-8.

It took . . . well, it took all that I have written here to teach me to be like Christ. And, praise God, He is not finished with me yet! He has much more to teach me to make me like the Savior. But I am growing. I know I am more like Jesus now than when I met Him.

When I was writing about the joy of having victory over my mothering trap, God gave me this Psalm.

> Psalm 34: "The man who knows the meaning of forgiveness, whose past failures no longer plague him, who stands blameless and guilt-free before God—that man is rich indeed . . . "

And then He reminded me that I had talked about our lives being full of struggles just like those of the people around us. But the struggles that Christians encounter can and will be so very different than those of non-believers because of His presence. And just knowing that helps us focus on the good that comes from the difficulties we face. Yes, there is a great difference for the man who knows forgiveness and the one who does not. Psalm 34 continues with:

> "The faithful and the faithless both suffer the uncertainties and insecurities of this life, but the child of God can depend always on the love of his Father. It is for this reason that there is light even in the midst of darkness, incomprehensible joy in the midst of sorrow, and

we can find a measure of happiness and well-being regardless of the circumstances that surround us."

I have realized that all of life is a choice. *We can choose to focus the bad or the good.* ". . . we can find a measure of happiness and well-being regardless of the circumstances that surround us."

I have two prayers for the rest of my life:
1. *I want to always look at circumstances with rejoicing.* If it is a bad experience, I can look for the lesson God is trying to teach me, to conform me more to the image of Jesus. If it is good, I can give double praise and thanks to God. I do need to remember that good and bad are present in every situation. I have the desire and will to choose to focus on the good. My prayer is that I will never turn from that desire.
2. *I want to finish well.* I want to be like Daniel, David, Isaac, Abraham, Paul, Peter, and Christ Himself. I do not want to be like Saul, Solomon, or Judas. These men were at one time disciples of God. They loved Him and wanted God's best for themselves. But somewhere along the way they got their eyes off the Master and onto themselves. Oh, God, keep me in Your way! Do not allow me to stray. I want to finish well.

EPILOGUE

The book you have just read was written in 1996. Upon publication, two more years had past. At that time I added a few facts, but now it is actually 22 years later! I will edit the original stories but add more up-dated facts. When I decided to have this work published again, I wanted to continue the story. But it will take a different format. After reading this story, my desire is that you continue reading the new book, *Loved By The Best*. It will tell in detail more of the following notes. God has led all the way and as we mature we can see it was all in His plan.

December 19, 1996, my mother went to be with the Lord. She had dreamed of Bible studies and more work in the community after Mike's homegoing. But just three months after his death, Mom was diagnosed with liver cancer. She was gone in seven weeks.

January 11, 1997, James and Gloria had a glorious wedding! They continue to grow in Christ and are becoming leaders at Lugogo Baptist Church. Today they have parented one boy and five girls! James has become a pastor and as a couple they disciple young couples. You will hear more of there fantastic journey in the next book.

August of 1997, all four of our children came to Uganda. Joe got to see where his wife calls home. We rode a launch in Queen Elizabeth Park where we saw hundreds of hippopotamuses, Cape buffalo, elephants, and many other animals. A highlight was a rafting trip down the mighty Nile River.

Nancy found a job in Kampala at the American Embassy while she was in Uganda in August. We were delighted with her presence for two years. When we came home July 19, 1999 for our "home assignment," Nancy left Uganda and moved to Philadelphia to be close to her sister and her husband. She worked in Charter Hospital there.

The hospital went bankrupt so Nancy lost her job. Due to her depression and mental health problems, she committed suicide November 16, 2000. Again there will be more of her story in the next book and how God helped us to handle the tragedy and again, use it for His glory.

Tim is still in San Francisco. He was taking youth to Texas to help build homes for the poor, teaching high school and university students to teach children in the inner city, and pastoring. He too has had many exciting adventures—a vow, a Masters in theology, becoming an excellent nurse, and much more.

Today Julie is a counselor in a unique school. It is one of three in the nation where all 500 students are challenged—wheelchairs, social issues, other physical issues, and depression.

Joe has graduated from Eastern, completed a computer-programming course, and continued working at Spirit and Truth Church in Philly. He now it the director of Information Technology at International Ministries in King of Prussia, PA. As a family they are attending a church near Pottstown, PA where they reside.

     Three boys have joined Joe and Julie Gonzalez — Noah, now 16; Ben, now 15, and Ethan 10. Delightful competent students/athletes and Grandma's delight.

     Jane Olaboro completed a two-year training course in catering and cooking. She is in charge of our guesthouse and doing a great job. Jane continues working for missionaries as their house help.

     April 20, 1998, the hip replacement I had had done in 1996 came apart. It happened on the tennis court! So, I had a second hip replacement. In 2002 I had the left hip replaced. Disaster of disasters, the right hip had 2 more replacements in 2006 and 2014 — now a total of FOUR! Also had to have the knee replaced so enjoy my crutches and recently a wheelchair.

The work in Uganda continues to grow and bless us. We are seeing marriages strengthened through couple's conferences. Childless couples are studying scriptures and finding that to be childless is not a sin. The Celebrate Kids programs are expanding so that now many more people are involved in the leadership. Have I ever said God is good? Well, if not, please, let me stay it: GOD IS GOOD!

For many more details and introductions, I trust you will read and enjoy *Loved By The Best*. Hopefully it will be on the market by the first of January. It has been a pleaure to review my life and to share it with the hundreds of people that have made our ministry possible. God bless you all.